At Issue

Should the Rich Pay Higher Taxes?

Other Books in the At Issue Series:

At Issue

Should the Rich Pay Higher Taxes?

Ronald D. Lankford Jr., Book Editor

GREENHAVEN PRESS
A part of Gale, Cengage Learning

GALE
CENGAGE Learning·

Detroit • New York • San Francisco • New Haven, Conn • Waterville, Maine • London

GALE
CENGAGE Learning·

Elizabeth Des Chenes, *Director, Content Strategy*
Cynthia Sanner, *Publisher*
Douglas Dentino, *Manager, New Product*

For more information, contact:
Greenhaven Press
27500 Drake Rd.
Farmington Hills, MI 48331-3535
Or you can visit our Internet site at gale.cengage.com

For product information and technology assistance, contact us at

Gale Customer Support, 1-800-877-4253
For permission to use material from this text or product, submit all requests online at www.cengage.com/permissions.

Further permissions questions can be e-mailed to permissionrequest@cengage.com.

Articles in Greenhaven Press anthologies are often edited for length to meet page require-ments. In addition, original titles of these works are changed to clearly present the main thesis and to explicitly indicate the author's opinion. Every effort is made to ensure that Greenhaven Press accurately reflects the original intent of the authors. Every effort has been made to trace the owners of copyrighted material.

Cover photograph copyright © Images.com/Corbis.

LIBRARY OF CONGRESS CATALOGING-IN-PUBLICATION DATA

Should the rich pay higher taxes? / Ronald D. Lankford Jr., book editor.
p. cm. -- (At issue)
Summary: "At Issue: Should the Rich Pay Higher Taxes? Books in this anthol-ogy series focus a wide range of viewpoints onto a single controversial issue, providing in-depth discussions by leading advocates, a quick grounding in the issues, and a challenge to critical thinking skills"-- Provided by publisher.
Includes bibliographical references and index.
ISBN 978-0-7377-6858-9 (hardback) -- ISBN 978-0-7377-6859-6 (paperback)
1. Rich people--Taxation--United States--Juvenile literature. I. Lankford, Ronald D., 1962-
HJ4653.R6S56 2014
336.20086'21--dc23
2012042413

Printed in the United States of America
1 2 3 4 5 6 7 18 17 16 15 14

Contents

Introduction

During the past several years, the debate over whether wealthy Americans should pay higher taxes has been revived. Republicans and Democrats, conservatives, liberals, and libertarians, have conducted a vigorous debate over who pays and who *should* pay taxes. While there seems to be little consensus over this issue, one thing is clear: The intensity and contentiousness of the argument has placed wealth and taxes at the center of the American political arena. Likewise, this debate has been replicated in many countries around the world.

While Americans have frequently debated tax policy, tax discussions—since 1980—have centered on lowering taxes on the wealthy. This famously began with President Ronald Reagan in 1980, with conservatives arguing that lower taxes on the rich would produce more revenue for state and federal governments. With lower taxes, the logic argued, fewer wealthy Americans would seek out tax shelters to avoid paying. The argument also asserted that lower taxes would encourage the wealthy to invest, helping to create more jobs.

Even during President George W. Bush's two terms in office (2001–2008), this logic—although not universally accepted—seemed to prevail. Lower taxes on all Americans, but especially on wealthier Americans, stimulated the economy. A question, then, arises. Why are many Americans now questioning the logic of this argument and suggesting that the wealthy should pay more taxes?

For many commentators and politicians, the answer is potentially twofold. First, the impact of the economic recession beginning in 2007–2008 may have shifted how many Americans view taxing the wealthy. And second, the falling off of revenue in the aftermath of the recession has spurred state and federal government to search for new funding sources.

In regard to attitudes toward the rich, Americans seem more willing to raise taxes since the recession began. In poll after poll, most Americans agree that the rich should be taxed at a higher rate. In a Pew Research poll from 2012, 58 percent believed that upper income Americans paid too little in taxes ($150,000 or more was perceived as wealthy in this survey). Likewise, 65 percent believed that the gap between the rich and poor was expanding. In relation to the recession, 42 percent believed that the upper class was in better shape *after* the downturn.

In a Gallup Poll survey from 2011, individuals were asked whether the rich should be taxed and the wealth redistributed. The results were split, with 47 percent choosing redistribution and 49 percent disagreeing. In a 2010 poll, 67 percent believed that the wealthy should pay more in Social Security taxes. Gallup, however, questioned the impact of the recession: In both instances, these results were similar to previous polls taken *before* the slump.

The findings of these polls, then, were mixed. While Americans may have been more willing to tax the wealthy, they continued to admire them. In fact, many hoped—one day—to become wealthy themselves. "Despite the recent political emphasis on wealth inequality and the call for higher taxes on the rich," noted Frank Newport of Gallup, "more than six in 10 Americans think the United States benefits from having a class of rich people, unchanged from 22 years ago."[1] While Americans may be more willing to tax the rich since the recession, there are clearly limits to how far this approach can be taken.

The second issue focused on the need to make up for lost revenue on the local, state, and federal government levels. Even while state revenues, to choose one example, were healthier in 2013 than they were in 2008 or 2009, levels of growth were much slower than before the recession began.

In 2012 the state of California voted for a new surcharge on the wealthiest earners as a way of shoring up education expenses. "At 13.3 percent," wrote Adam Nagourney in the *New York Times*, "the top-tier California income tax is, in addition to being higher than any other state, the steepest it has been since World War II."[2] Californians approved Governor Jerry Brown's measure on November 7, 2012, by 54 percent, despite what opponents considered a steep hike for the state's rich taxpayers.

In March 2013, the state of New York proposed similar legislation. Governor Andrew Cuomo argued that the tax hike would be a "short-term solution" for the current financial emergency. While the suggested legislation remains controversial, other states such as Minnesota also are considering new tax measures focused on the wealthy. "I think partly there's some recognition that the level of income inequality has grown, and the level of income inequality has especially grown in places like California and New York," noted Kim Rueben of the Tax Policy Center.[3]

As noted, these debates are taking place around the world. At the beginning of 2013, politicians in India joined those in Britain, Australia, and the United States in discussing new ways to raise revenue. "Like gilded bowling pins against the rolling forces of global populism," noted Robert Frank at CNBC, "the long-favorable tax policies for the wealthy are rapidly falling one by one."[4]

Taxing the wealthy—in America and elsewhere—remains a contentious issue. If Americans remain conflicted, this partly rests on the fact that the poor and middle class wish, one day, to take their place among the wealthy. Despite this conflict, the poor and middle class generally seem more willing to raise taxes on the rich than they did before the recession.

Likewise, legislators seem more willing to exploit this class conflict as they search for new taxes in the face of falling revenue since the recession began. While the aftershock of the recession may not be the only reason for the new prominence of the debate over taxing the wealthy, the repercussions have given the debate a higher profile.

The contributors to *At Issue: Should the Rich Pay Higher Taxes?* examine this issue from a variety of angles, including tax loopholes, the federal deficit, and taxation in relation to improving the economy.

Notes

1. Frank Newport, "Americans Like Having a Rich Class, as They Did 22 Years Ago," Gallup, May 11, 2012. http://www.gallup.com/poll/154619/Americans-Having-Rich-Class-Years-Ago.aspx.
2. Adam Nagourney, "Two-Tax Rise Tests Wealthy in California," *New York Times*, February 6, 2013.
3. Thomas Kaplan, "Deal in Albany Would Extend Higher Taxes on Top Earners," *New York Times*, March 20, 2013.
4. Robert Frank, "India Joins the Debate Over Taxing the Rich," CNBC, January 16, 2013. http://www.cnbc.com/id/100385307.

1

The Rich Should Pay Higher Taxes

David Cay Johnston

David Cay Johnston teaches at Syracuse University College of Law and Whitman School of Management.

During the past thirty years, Americans have conducted an experiment in reducing taxes for the wealthy. Instead of helping the working class, however, this policy has left these Americans with a greater tax burden. Even those who pay no federal tax pay many other taxes (food, gas, property), while many rich Americans pay no taxes at all. As working-class Americans have assumed more of the tax burden, wealthy Americans have grown wealthier. These changes underline the belief that American tax policy since President Ronald Reagan has been a failure.

For three decades we have conducted a massive economic experiment, testing a theory known as supply-side economics. The theory goes like this: Lower tax rates will encourage more investment, which in turn will mean more jobs and greater prosperity—so much so that tax revenues will go up, despite lower rates. The late Milton Friedman, the libertarian economist who wanted to shut down public parks because he considered them socialism, promoted this strategy. Ronald Reagan embraced Friedman's ideas and made them into policy when he was elected president in 1980.

For the past decade, we have doubled down on this theory of supply-side economics with the tax cuts sponsored by President George W. Bush in 2001 and 2003, which President Obama has agreed to continue for two years.

You would think that whether this grand experiment worked would be settled after three decades. You would think the practitioners of the dismal science of economics would look at their demand curves and the data on incomes and taxes and pronounce a verdict, the way Galileo and Copernicus did when they showed that geocentrism was a fantasy because Earth revolves around the sun (known as heliocentrism). But economics is not like that. It is not like physics with its laws and arithmetic with its absolute values.

Tax policy is something the framers left to politics. And in politics, the facts often matter less than who has the biggest bullhorn.

The Mad Men who once ran campaigns featuring doctors extolling the health benefits of smoking are now busy marketing the dogma that tax cuts mean broad prosperity, no matter what the facts show.

As millions of Americans prepare to file their annual taxes, they do so in an environment of media-perpetuated tax myths. Here are a few points about taxes and the economy that you may not know, to consider as you prepare to file your taxes. (All figures are inflation-adjusted.). . .

1. *Poor Americans do pay taxes.*

Gretchen Carlson, the Fox News host, said last year "47 percent of Americans don't pay any taxes." John McCain and Sarah Palin both said similar things during the 2008 campaign about the bottom half of Americans.

Ari Fleischer, the former Bush White House spokesman, once said "50 percent of the country gets benefits without paying for them."

Actually, they pay lots of taxes—just not lots of federal income taxes.

Data from the Tax Foundation show that in 2008, the average income for the bottom half of taxpayers was $15,300.

This year [2011] the first $9,350 of income is exempt from taxes for singles and $18,700 for married couples, just slightly more than in 2008. That means millions of the poor do not make enough to owe income taxes.

But they still pay plenty of other taxes, including federal payroll taxes. Between gas taxes, sales taxes, utility taxes and other taxes, no one lives tax-free in America.

> *Between gas taxes, sales taxes, utility taxes and other taxes, no one lives tax-free in America.*

When it comes to state and local taxes, the poor bear a heavier burden than the rich in every state except Vermont, the Institute on Taxation and Economic Policy calculated from official data. In Alabama, for example, the burden on the poor is more than twice that of the top 1 percent. The one-fifth of Alabama families making less than $13,000 pay almost 11 percent of their income in state and local taxes, compared with less than 4 percent for those who make $229,000 or more. . . .

2. *The wealthiest Americans don't carry the burden.*

This is one of those oft-used canards [false beliefs]. Sen. Rand Paul, the tea party favorite from Kentucky, told [talk show host] David Letterman recently that "the wealthy do pay most of the taxes in this country."

The Internet is awash with statements that the top 1 percent pays, depending on the year, 38 percent or more than 40 percent of taxes.

It's true that the top 1 percent of wage earners paid 38 percent of the federal income taxes in 2008 (the most recent year for which data is available). But people forget that the income tax is less than half of federal taxes and only one-fifth of taxes at all levels of government.

Despite skyrocketing incomes, the federal tax burden on the richest 400 has been slashed.

Social Security, Medicare and unemployment insurance taxes (known as payroll taxes) are paid mostly by the bottom 90 percent of wage earners. That's because, once you reach $106,800 of income, you pay no more for Social Security, though the much smaller Medicare tax applies to all wages. [Billionaire businessman] Warren Buffett pays the exact same amount of Social Security taxes as someone who earns $106,800....

3. *In fact, the wealthy are paying less taxes.*

The Internal Revenue Service [IRS] issues an annual report on the 400 highest income-tax payers. In 1961, there were 398 taxpayers who made $1 million or more, so I compared their income tax burdens from that year to 2007.

Despite skyrocketing incomes, the federal tax burden on the richest 400 has been slashed, thanks to a variety of loopholes, allowable deductions and other tools. The actual share of their income paid in taxes, according to the IRS, is 16.6 percent. Adding payroll taxes barely nudges that number.

Compare that to the vast majority of Americans, whose share of their income going to federal taxes increased from 13.1 percent in 1961 to 22.5 percent in 2007.

(By the way, during seven of the eight George W. Bush years, the IRS report on the top 400 taxpayers was labeled a state secret, a policy that the Obama administration overturned almost instantly after his inauguration.)...

4. *Many of the very richest pay no current income taxes at all.*

John Paulson, the most successful hedge-fund manager of all, bet against the mortgage market one year and then bet with [talk show host] Glenn Beck in the gold market the next. Paulson made himself $9 billion in fees in just two years. His current tax bill on that $9 billion? Zero.

Congress lets hedge-fund managers earn all they can now and pay their taxes years from now.

In 2007, Congress debated whether hedge-fund managers should pay the top tax rate that applies to wages, bonuses and other compensation for their labors, which is 35 percent. That tax rate starts at about $300,000 of taxable income—not even pocket change to Paulson, but almost 12 years of gross pay to the median-wage worker.

The Republicans and a key Democrat, Sen. Charles Schumer of New York, fought to keep the tax rate on hedge-fund managers at 15 percent, arguing that the profits from hedge funds should be considered capital gains, not ordinary income, which got a lot of attention in the news.

What the news media missed is that hedge-fund managers don't even pay 15 percent. At least, not currently. So long as they leave their money, known as "carried interest," in the hedge fund, their taxes are deferred. They only pay taxes when they cash out, which could be decades from now for younger managers. How do these hedge-fund managers get money in the meantime? By borrowing against the carried interest, often at absurdly low rates—currently about 2 percent.

Lots of other people live tax-free, too. I have [business person] Donald Trump's tax records for four years early in his career. He paid no taxes for two of those years. Big real-estate investors enjoy tax-free living under a 1993 law President Clinton signed. It lets "professional" real-estate investors use paper losses like depreciation on their buildings against any cash income, even if they end up with negative incomes like Trump.

Frank and Jamie McCourt, who own the Los Angeles Dodgers, have not paid any income taxes since at least 2004, their divorce case revealed. Yet they spent $45 million one year alone. How? They just borrowed against Dodger ticket revenue and other assets. To the IRS, they look like paupers.

In Wisconsin, Terrence Wall, who unsuccessfully sought the Republican nomination for U.S. Senate in 2010, paid no income taxes on as much as $14 million of recent income, his disclosure forms showed. Asked about his living tax-free while working people pay taxes, he had a simple response: Everyone should pay less. . . .

5. *And (surprise!) since Reagan, only the wealthy have gained significant income.*

The Heritage Foundation, the Cato Institute and similar conservative marketing organizations tell us relentlessly that lower tax rates will make us all better off.

"When tax rates are reduced, the economy's growth rate improves and living standards increase," according to Daniel J. Mitchell, an economist at Heritage until he joined Cato. He says that supply-side economics is "the simple notion that lower tax rates will boost work, saving, investment and entrepreneurship."

When Reagan was elected president, the top marginal tax rate (the tax rate paid on the last dollar of income earned) was 70 percent. He cut it to 50 percent and then 28 percent starting in 1987. It was raised by George H.W. Bush and Clinton, and then cut by George W. Bush. The top rate is now 35 percent.

Since 1980, when Reagan won the presidency promising prosperity through tax cuts, the average income of the vast majority—the bottom 90 percent of Americans—has increased a meager $303, or 1 percent. Put another way, for each dollar people in the vast majority made in 1980, in 2008 their income was up to $1.01.

Those at the top did better. The top 1 percent's average income more than doubled to $1.1 million, according to an analysis of tax data by economists Thomas Piketty and Emmanuel Saez. The really rich, the top one-tenth of 1 percent, each enjoyed almost $4 in 2008 for each dollar in 1980.

Despite all the noise that America has the world's second-highest corporate tax rate, the actual taxes paid by corporations are falling.

The top 300,000 Americans now enjoy almost as much income as the bottom 150 million, the data show. . . .

6. *When it comes to corporations, the story is much the same—less taxes.*

Corporate profits in 2008, the latest year for which data are available, were $1,830 billion, up almost 12 percent from $1,638.7 billion in 2000. Yet, even though corporate tax rates have not been cut, corporate income-tax revenues fell to $230 billion from $249 billion—an 8 percent decline, thanks to a number of loopholes. The official 2010 profit numbers are not added up and released by the government, but the amount paid in corporate taxes is: In 2010 they fell further, to $191 billion—a decline of more than 23 percent compared with 2000.

7. *Some corporate tax breaks destroy jobs.*

Despite all the noise that America has the world's second-highest corporate tax rate, the actual taxes paid by corporations are falling because of the growing number of loopholes and companies shifting profits to tax havens like the Cayman Islands.

And right now America's corporations are sitting on close to $2 trillion in cash that is not being used to build factories, create jobs or anything else, but acts as an insurance policy for managers unwilling to take the risk of actually building the businesses they are paid so well to run. That cash hoard, by the way, works out to nearly $13,000 per taxpaying household.

A corporate tax rate that is too low actually destroys jobs. That's because a higher tax rate encourages businesses (who don't want to pay taxes) to keep the profits in the business and reinvest, rather than pull them out as profits and have to pay high taxes.

The 2004 American Jobs Creation Act, which passed with bipartisan support, allowed more than 800 companies to bring profits that were untaxed but overseas back to the United States. Instead of paying the usual 35 percent tax, the companies paid just 5.25 percent.

The companies said bringing the money home—"repatriating" it, they called it—would mean lots of jobs. Sen. John Ensign, the Nevada Republican, put the figure at 660,000 new jobs.

President Reagan signed into law 11 tax increases, targeted at people down the income ladder.

Pfizer, the drug company, was the biggest beneficiary. It brought home $37 billion, saving $11 billion in taxes. Almost immediately it started firing people. Since the law took effect, Pfizer has let 40,000 workers go. In all, it appears that at least 100,000 jobs were destroyed.

Now Congressional Republicans and some Democrats are gearing up again to pass another tax holiday, promoting a new Jobs Creation Act. It would affect 10 times as much money as the 2004 law. . . .

8. Republicans like taxes too.

President Reagan signed into law 11 tax increases, targeted at people down the income ladder. His administration and the Washington press corps called the increases "revenue enhancers." Reagan raised Social Security taxes so high that by the end of 2008, the government had collected more than $2 *trillion* in surplus tax.

George W. Bush signed a tax increase, too, in 2006, despite his written ironclad pledge never to raise taxes on anyone. It raised taxes on teenagers by requiring kids up to age 17, who earned money, to pay taxes at their parents' tax rate, which would almost always be higher than the rate they would otherwise pay. It was a story that ran buried inside *The New York Times* one Sunday, but nowhere else.

In fact, thanks to Republicans, one in three Americans will pay higher taxes this year than they did last year.

First, some history. In 2009, President Obama pushed his own tax cut—for the working class. He persuaded Congress to enact the Making Work Pay Tax Credit. Over the two years 2009 and 2010, it saved single workers up to $800 and married heterosexual couples up to $1,600, even if only one spouse worked. The top 5 percent or so of taxpayers were denied this tax break.

The Obama administration called it "the biggest middle-class tax cut" ever. Yet last December the Republicans, poised to regain control of the House of Representatives, killed Obama's Making Work Pay Credit while extending the Bush tax cuts for two more years—a policy Obama agreed to.

By doing so, Congressional Republican leaders increased taxes on a third of Americans, virtually all of them the working poor, this year.

As a result, of the 155 million households in the tax system, 51 million will pay an average of $129 more this year. That is $6.6 billion in higher taxes for the working poor, the nonpartisan Tax Policy Center estimated.

In addition, the Republicans changed the rate of workers' FICA [Federal Insurance Contributions Act] contributions, which finances half of Social Security. The result:

If you are single and make less than $20,000, or married and less than $40,000, you lose under this plan. But the top 5 percent, people who make more than $106,800, will save $2,136 ($4,272 for two-career couples). . . .

9. *Other countries do it better.*

We measure our economic progress, and our elected leaders debate tax policy, in terms of a crude measure known as gross domestic product. The way the official statistics are put together, each dollar spent buying solar energy equipment counts the same as each dollar spent investigating murders.

We do not give any measure of value to time spent rearing children or growing our own vegetables or to time off for leisure and community service.

And we do not measure the economic damage done by shocks, such as losing a job, which means not only loss of income and depletion of savings, but loss of health insurance, which a Harvard Medical School study found results in 45,000 unnecessary deaths each year.

Compare this to Germany, one of many countries with a smarter tax system and smarter spending policies.

Germans work less, make more per hour and get much better parental leave than Americans, many of whom get no fringe benefits such as health care, pensions or even a retirement savings plan. By many measures the vast majority live better in Germany than in America.

To achieve this, unmarried Germans on average pay 52 percent of their income in taxes. Americans average 30 percent, according to the Organization for Economic Cooperation and Development.

At first blush the German tax burden seems horrendous. But in Germany (as well as in Britain, France, Scandinavia, Canada, Australia and Japan), tax-supported institutions provide many of the things Americans pay for with after-tax dollars. Buying wholesale rather than retail saves money.

A proper comparison would take the 30 percent average tax on American workers and add their out-of-pocket spending on health care, college tuition and fees for services, and compare that with taxes that the average German pays. Add it all up and the combination of tax and personal spending is roughly equal in both countries, but with a large risk of catastrophic loss in America, and a tiny risk in Germany.

Americans take on $85 billion of debt each year for higher education, while college is financed by taxes in Germany and tuition is cheap to free in other modern countries. While soaring medical costs are a key reason that since 1980 bankruptcy in America has increased 15 times faster than population growth, no one in Germany or the rest of the modern world goes broke because of accident or illness. And child poverty in America is the highest among modern countries—almost twice the rate in Germany, which is close to the average of modern countries.

On the corporate tax side, the Germans encourage reinvestment at home and the outsourcing of low-value work, like auto assembly, and German rules tightly control accounting so that profits earned at home cannot be made to appear as profits earned in tax havens.

Adopting the German system is not the answer for America. But crafting a tax system that benefits the vast majority, reduces risks, provides universal health care and focuses on diplomacy rather than militarism abroad (and at home) would be a lot smarter than what we have now.

Here is a question to ask yourself: We started down this road with Reagan's election in 1980 and upped the ante in this century with George W. Bush.

How long does it take to conclude that a policy has failed to fulfill its promises? And as you think of that, keep in mind George Washington. When he fell ill his doctors followed the common wisdom of the era. They cut him and bled him to remove bad blood. As Washington's condition grew worse, they bled him more. And like the mantra of tax cuts for the rich, they kept applying the same treatment until they killed him.

Luckily we don't bleed the sick anymore, but we are bleeding our government to death.

2

The Rich Should Not Pay Higher Taxes

Curtis S. Dubay

Curtis S. Dubay is a senior analyst in tax policy in the Thomas A. Roe Institute for Economic Policy Studies at The Heritage Foundation.

During Barack Obama's presidency, taxes have risen, further damaging a recessed American economy. Unfortunately, there are a number of myths suggesting that taxing the rich at higher rates will lead to a recovery. For instance, many believe that the rich do not pay their fair share of taxes and that raising taxes on the rich will help close the deficit. In truth, the rich pay the majority of federal taxes and raising their taxes will only deepen the economic recession. If the president and Congress hope to create a healthier economy, taxes should be lowered for everyone.

President Barack Obama plans to raise the top two income tax rates from their current 33 and 35 percent levels to 36 and 39.6 percent, respectively. This would undo the 2001 and 2003 tax cuts for Americans earning more than $250,000 ($200,000 for singles) and return the top rates to the levels of 1993 to 2000 during the Clinton Administration.

In addition to these tax hikes, the House of Representatives' Ways and Means Committee, led by Chairman Charlie Rangel (D-NY), favors another tax to fund the government takeover of the health care system. The "Rangel plan" would levy a 1 percent surtax for married couples earning between $350,000 and $500,000 a year, a 1.5 percent surtax on couple incomes between $500,000 and $1,000,000, and a 5.4 percent surtax for couples earning more than $1,000,000. For singles, the surtax would kick in for earners making more than $280,000 a year, $400,000, and $800,000, respectively. It would be phased in beginning in 2011 and could rise higher in future years if Congress decides it needs more revenue to fund its government-run health care system. Contrary to arguments made by proponents of these tax hikes, tax increases in the early 1990s did not lift the economy to the highs experienced later in the decade.

President Obama's and Chairman Rangel's tax hikes would increase the progressivity of the already highly progressive tax code. High-income earners pay substantially higher tax rates than do lower-income earners. If passed, this increased progressivity will damage economic growth by lowering the incentives to work, save, and invest. This will stifle job creation, further slowing the growth of already stagnant wages.

Those who support this tax increase point to several arguments to boost their case. But when these arguments are scrutinized, it is clear they do not hold up. Tax hikes on the rich will not balance the budget or close deficits. High earners already have a vast majority of the federal income tax burden, and the proposed tax hikes will badly damage the economy at a time when it cannot absorb any new negative shocks.

The President should scrap his plan to hike the top two income tax rates and Chairman Rangel his plan to pile additional tax hikes on high earners. Instead, they should propose to immediately cut spending, including reforming entitlement programs, and extending the 2001 and 2003 tax cuts for all taxpayers. Additionally, they should propose further *cutting* tax rates to help the ailing economy.

Myth 1: Raising taxes on the rich will close budget deficits.

Truth: Increasing the progressivity of the income tax code by raising the top two rates will not close the deficit. In fact, it will lead to more revenue volatility, which will lead to large future deficits.

A progressive income tax system collects increasing amounts of revenue during periods of economic growth and decreasing revenue during downturns. It does so mostly because of the volatility of high earners' incomes. During periods of economic growth, their incomes rise sharply and they pay increasingly higher taxes. But because much of high earners' income stems from volatile sources, such as capital gains, dividends, business income, and bonuses, their incomes fall just as sharply during economic downturns as they rose during good economic times and they have less income to be taxed.

Unless Congress suddenly develops spending restraint, increasing the progressivity of the tax code will only amplify the volatility of revenue fluctuations and increase future deficits. When revenue increases, mostly from high earners, during periods of economic growth, spending would increase because Congress cannot resist spending additional money. But, as history shows, when economic growth slows and revenues fall, Congress does not cut back on its spending largesse. Larger deficits would occur because the gap between spending and revenue would grow compared to previous recessionary periods.

The top 20 percent of all income earners pay a substantial majority of all federal taxes.

Even if Congress ignores the long-term implications of more volatility and decides to close the deficits by raising taxes instead of borrowing as it is doing currently, it still cannot do it just by taxing more of high earners' income. Congress would have to decide to raise top rates to levels most

Americans would consider confiscatory. In 2006, the latest year of available data, there was $2.2 trillion of taxable income for taxpayers earning more than $200,000. Assuming the amount of income at that level is similar this year, Congress would need to tax 80 percent of that income in order to close the projected $1.8 trillion deficit. Tax rates at such levels would significantly decrease economic activity and taxpayers would likely avoid or evade paying them so the revenue gains would likely never materialize.

Myth 2: The rich do not pay their fair share.

Truth: The top 20 percent of income earners pay almost all federal taxes.

The top 20 percent of all income earners pay a substantial majority of all federal taxes. According to the Congressional Budget Office (CBO), in 2006, the latest year of available data, the top 20 percent of income earners paid almost 70 percent of all federal taxes. This share was 4 percent higher than in 2000, before the 2001 and 2003 tax cuts.

It is hard to see how the rich benefit from a tax code they pay almost exclusively.

When only looking at income taxes, the share of the top 20 percent increases even further. In 2006, the top 20 percent paid 86.3 percent of all income taxes. This was an increase of 6 percent from 2000.

Myth 3: The income tax code favors the rich and well-connected.

Truth: The bottom 50 percent of income earners pay almost no income taxes and the poor and middle-income earners benefit greatly from the tax code.

This widely propagated myth has found its way to the White House Web site's tax page: "For too long, the U.S. tax code has benefited the wealthy and well-connected at the expense of the vast majority of Americans."

As shown in myth number 2, the top 20 percent pay almost 70 percent of all federal taxes and over 86 percent of all income taxes. It is hard to see how the rich benefit from a tax code they pay almost exclusively.

The bottom 40 percent of all income earners benefit greatly from the income tax code. In fact, they actually pay negative income tax rates because refundable credits, such as the Child Tax Credit and the Earned Income Tax Credit (EITC), wipe out their tax liability and pay out more money to them than they ever paid in.

Because of refundable credits, a family of four in the bottom 20 percent of income earners paid an effective income tax rate of −6.6 percent in 2006. As a result, such a family received $1,300 through the tax code. A family of four in the second-lowest 20 percent of income earners paid an effective tax rate of −0.8 percent and received $408 of income through the tax code.

The stimulus bill created a new refundable credit and expanded three others. This will further reduce the income tax burden of low-income earners, to the extent they can pay less, and increase the income they receive through the tax code.

The tax code should collect revenue in the least economically damaging way possible.

The income tax burden of low-income earners has trended down for years. In 2006, the bottom 50 percent of all income tax filers paid only 2.99 percent of all income taxes. This was down 57 percent from 1980 levels, when the bottom 50 percent paid 7 percent.

Altogether, historical trends and the recent tax policies in the stimulus likely mean that when the data for recent years is released, the bottom 50 percent of all taxpayers will have paid no income taxes whatsoever.

Myth 4: It is all right to raise tax rates on the rich—they can afford it.

Truth: Just because someone can afford to pay higher taxes does not mean he should be forced to do so.

The faulty principle of "ability to pay" holds that those who earn more should pay proportionally more taxes because they can afford to do so. Such thinking can be a slippery slope because, technically, virtually anyone can afford to pay more taxes. The ability-to-pay principle has no grounding in economics, as it relies on a completely subjective judgment of fairness.

The tax code should collect revenue in the least economically damaging way possible. Raising rates on the rich damages economic growth because it reduces the incentives to work, save, invest, and accept economic risk—the ingredients necessary for economic growth.

Raising taxes on the rich hurts workers at all income levels—especially low- and middle-income earners. The rich are the most likely to invest. Their investment allows new businesses to get off the ground or existing businesses to expand. This creates new jobs and raises wages for Americans at all income levels. Taxing more of their income transfers money to Congress that they could otherwise have invested. This means the economy forgoes new jobs and higher wages that the investment would have created for less effective government spending.

There is a tax code that can collect more from the high earners than from the lower earners without being a barrier to economic growth: Under a flat tax, a taxpayer who earns 100 percent more than another taxpayer pays 100 percent more taxes, but faces no disincentive to earn more since he will pay the same rate on every additional dollar earned.

Myth 5: Higher tax rates in the 1990s did not hurt economic growth, so it is all right to raise them to those levels again.

Truth: High tax rates in the 1990s were a contributing factor to the 2001 recession and returning to those rates will damage the already severely weakened economy.

The economy boomed during the 1990s for a number of reasons. One key factor was an advance in information technology. Computers, cell phones, the Internet, and other technological advances made businesses more efficient. This increased profits and wages and created numerous new jobs.

The 1997 tax cut that lowered tax rates on dividends and capital gains from 28 to 20 percent was also a major factor helping fuel the economic growth of this period. It strengthened the already strong gains from the technology boom. The impressive growth of the S&P 500 index after its passage is testimony to that fact. In the year before the tax cut, the S&P 500 index increased by 22 percent. In the following year, it increased by more than 40 percent.

The economic benefits of the technological advances and lower taxes on investment were strong enough to overcome the negative impact of the higher income tax rates and the economy exhibited impressive growth—initially. Even though the economy overcame high income tax rates temporarily, it was not strong enough to resist their negative pull forever:

> A contributing factor to the 2001 recession was the oppressively high levels of federal tax extracted from the economy. In the 40 years prior to 2000, federal tax receipts averaged about 18.2 percent of gross domestic product (GDP). In 1998 and 1999, the tax share stood at 20.0 percent, and in 2000, it shot up to tie the previous record of 20.9 percent set in 1944 [J.D. Foster, "The Tax Relief Program Worked: Make the Tax Cuts Permanent," Heritage Foundation Backgrounder, No. 2145, June 18, 2008].

Taxes were high because the top income tax rates were 39.6 percent and 36 percent—the same rates President Obama and Congress now target.

The economy is in a much more precarious position now than it was in the 1990s. In June 2009 alone the economy lost 467,000 jobs. With no new innovations like those that created economic growth in the 1990s on the horizon to jump-start growth today, the economy simply cannot afford tax policies that will destroy more jobs and make it more difficult for the economy to recover.

Myth 6: The 2001 and 2003 tax cuts did not generate strong economic growth.

Truth: The tax cuts generated strong economic growth.

The 2001 and 2003 tax cuts generated strong economic growth. The 2003 cuts, however, were more effective at creating economic growth because Congress designed them expressly for that purpose. They worked better because they increased the incentives to generate new income by accelerating the phase-in of the 2001 reduction in marginal income tax rates, and by reducing rates on capital gains and dividends, lowering the cost of capital which is critical for economic recovery and growth.

Lower income tax rates generally promote growth, but since the 2001 cuts were phased in over several years, they did not kick in quickly enough to change the behavior of workers, businesses, and investors to help boost the ailing economy, so growth remained sluggish. The 2001 cuts also increased the Child Tax Credit from $500 to $1,000 a child. Although a large tax cut from a revenue perspective, the increase in the Child Tax Credit did nothing to increase growth-promoting incentives. Recognizing that the slow phase-in of rate reductions was not generating economic growth, Congress accelerated the rate reductions to increase the incentives to work, save, and invest during the 2003 cuts.

The 2003 tax cuts also lowered rates on capital gains and dividends, generating strong growth by decreasing the cost of capital, which caused investment to increase. More investment meant that more money was available for start-up capital for

new businesses and for existing businesses to expand opera-
tions and add new jobs. The rate cuts on capital gains and
dividends also unlocked capital trapped in investments that
paid lower returns than otherwise could have been earned if
the tax did not exist. This generated economic growth by allowing capital to flow freely to its most efficient use.

The increased incentives to save and invest, coupled with
an acceleration of the cuts on marginal income tax rates, were
a major reason economic growth picked up steam almost immediately after the 2003 tax cuts:

> The passage of [the 2003 tax cuts] started a different story.
> In the first quarter of that year, real GDP [Gross Domestic
> Product] grew at a pedestrian 1.2 percent. In the second
> quarter, during which [the 2003 cuts were] signed into law,
> economic growth jumped to 3.5 percent, the fastest growth
> since the previous decade. In the third quarter, the rate of
> growth jumped again to an astounding 7.5 percent [Foster,
> 2008].

Unfortunately, President Obama and Congress plan to increase the income tax rates and taxes on capital gains and
dividends. This would reverse the beneficial effects of the 2001
and 2003 cuts and further slow economic growth during this
severe recession.

*Myth 7: Raising the top two income tax rates will not nega-
tively impact small businesses because only 2 percent of them
pay rates at that level.*

*Truth: Raising the top two income tax rates will negatively
impact almost three-fourths of all economic activity created by
small businesses.*

Small businesses are a vital component of the economy.
They create jobs for millions of Americans and are a major
factor driving economic growth.

Evaluating tax policy on the number of small businesses
that pay the top two rates is not the proper way to determine
the impact of raising those rates. What is important is how

much small-business income is subject to the top two rates. This measures the extent to which the top two rates affect the economic activity that small businesses create.

Using this more accurate metric, it is clear that the top two rates have an enormous impact on small businesses. According to the Treasury Department, 72 percent of small business income is subject to those rates.

Highly successful small businesses faced with higher tax rates will cut back on plans to expand.

The amount of small business income subject to the top two rates is high in relation to the number of businesses that pay the rates because these businesses are the most successful. As a result they employ the most people and generate the most economic activity.

Raising rates on these successful businesses would damage the economy at any time, but doing so now will only cost more people their jobs. Highly successful small businesses faced with higher tax rates will cut back on plans to expand, hire fewer workers, and lower wages for current workers at a time when the economy desperately needs them to expand and create more jobs.

Higher rates also discourage would-be entrepreneurs from entering the market. This will negatively affect long-term economic growth because businesses that otherwise would have been created and added jobs to the economy will never get off the starting blocks.

Distorting the Facts

The many arguments used by proponents of higher taxes ignore basic economic facts and distort the positive benefits of the 2001 and 2003 tax cuts.

The truth is that the 2001 and 2003 tax cuts were a major factor behind robust economic growth between 2003 and

2007. Undoing those tax cuts now for any taxpayers would inflict unnecessary damage to a struggling economy and needlessly cost many more Americans their jobs.

Adding additional higher surtaxes on high earners to fund a government takeover of the health care system would only do more damage to the economy and lead to more lost jobs and lower economic growth.

Instead of imposing these economy-injuring tax hikes, Congress should close budget deficits and spur economic growth by:

- Immediately cutting spending, including reforming the Social Security, Medicare, and Medicaid entitlement programs, in order to get long-term budget deficits under control;

- Making the 2001 and 2003 tax cuts permanent for all taxpayers; and

- Further cutting tax rates on workers and investors.

Raising taxes on the rich will hurt the economy at a time when the U.S. can least afford further damage.

3

The Warren Buffett Rule
Would Equalize Taxation

Warren E. Buffett

Warren E. Buffett is the chairman and chief executive of Berkshire Hathaway.

For too long, the US Congress has coddled the super-rich with a low tax rate. Percentage-wise, the wealthy pay fewer taxes than anyone else. When taxes on the rich were higher, however, the American economy was healthier. The super-rich remain committed to America and will not stop investing because of higher tax rates. It is time for the Congress to make the wealthy pay their fair share.

Suppose that an investor you admire and trust comes to you with an investment idea. "This is a good one," he says enthusiastically. "I'm in it, and I think you should be, too."

Would your reply possibly be this? "Well, it all depends on what my tax rate will be on the gain you're saying we're going to make. If the taxes are too high, I would rather leave the money in my savings account, earning a quarter of 1 percent." Only in Grover Norquist's [political advocate who opposes all taxes] imagination does such a response exist.

Between 1951 and 1954, when the capital gains rate was 25 percent and marginal rates on dividends reached 91 percent in extreme cases, I sold securities and did pretty wel the years from 1956 to 1969, the top marginal rate fell modestly, but was still a lofty 70 percent—and the tax rate on capital gains inched up to 27.5 percent. I was managing funds for investors then. Never did anyone mention taxes as a reason to forgo an investment opportunity that I offered.

The group's average income in 2009 was $202 million— which works out to a "wage" of $97,000 per hour, based on a 40-hour workweek.

Under those burdensome rates, moreover, both employment and the gross domestic product [G.D.P.] (a measure of the nation's economic output) increased at a rapid clip. The middle class and the rich alike gained ground.

So let's forget about the rich and ultrarich going on strike and stuffing their ample funds under their mattresses if— gasp—capital gains rates and ordinary income rates are increased. The ultrarich, including me, will forever pursue investment opportunities.

And, wow, do we have plenty to invest. The Forbes 400, the wealthiest individuals in America, hit a new group record for wealth this year: $1.7 trillion. That's more than five times the $300 billion total in 1992. In recent years, my gang has been leaving the middle class in the dust.

A huge tail wind from tax cuts has pushed us along. In 1992, the tax paid by the 400 highest incomes in the United States (a different universe from the Forbes list) averaged 26.4 percent of adjusted gross income. In 2009, the most recent year reported, the rate was 19.9 percent. It's nice to have friends in high places.

Under-Taxing the Rich

The group's average income in 2009 was $202 million—which works out to a "wage" of $97,000 per hour, based on a 40-

hour workweek. (I'm assuming they're paid during lunch hours.) Yet more than a quarter of these ultrawealthy paid less than 15 percent of their take in combined federal income and payroll taxes. Half of this crew paid less than 20 percent. And—brace yourself—a few actually paid nothing.

We need Congress, right now, to enact a minimum tax on high incomes.

This outrage points to the necessity for more than a simple revision in upper-end tax rates, though that's the place to start. I support President Obama's proposal to eliminate the Bush tax cuts for high-income taxpayers. However, I prefer a cutoff point somewhat above $250,000—maybe $500,000 or so.

Additionally, we need Congress, right now, to enact a minimum tax on high incomes. I would suggest 30 percent of taxable income between $1 million and $10 million, and 35 percent on amounts above that. A plain and simple rule like that will block the efforts of lobbyists, lawyers and contribution-hungry legislators to keep the ultrarich paying rates well below those incurred by people with income just a tiny fraction of ours. Only a minimum tax on very high incomes will prevent the stated tax rate from being eviscerated by these warriors for the wealthy.

Above all, we should not postpone these changes in the name of "reforming" the tax code. True, changes are badly needed. We need to get rid of arrangements like "carried interest" that enable income from labor to be magically converted into capital gains. And it's sickening that a Cayman Islands mail drop can be central to tax maneuvering by wealthy individuals and corporations.

But the reform of such complexities should not promote delay in our correcting simple and expensive inequities. We can't let those who want to protect the privileged get away with insisting that we do nothing until we can do everything.

Our government's goal should be to bring in revenues of 18.5 percent of G.D.P. and spend about 21 percent of G.D.P.—levels that have been attained over extended periods in the past and can clearly be reached again. As the math makes clear, this won't stem our budget deficits; in fact, it will continue them. But assuming even conservative projections about inflation and economic growth, this ratio of revenue to spending will keep America's debt stable in relation to the country's economic output.

In the last fiscal year, we were far away from this fiscal balance—bringing in 15.5 percent of G.D.P. in revenue and spending 22.4 percent. Correcting our course will require major concessions by both Republicans and Democrats.

All of America is waiting for Congress to offer a realistic and concrete plan for getting back to this fiscally sound path. Nothing less is acceptable.

In the meantime, maybe you'll run into someone with a terrific investment idea, who won't go forward with it because of the tax he would owe when it succeeds. Send him my way. Let me unburden him.

4

The Warren Buffett Rule Would Not Equalize Taxation

Curtis S. Dubay

Curtis S. Dubay is a senior analyst in tax policy in the Thomas A. Roe Institute for Economic Policy Studies at The Heritage Foundation.

In insisting that the rich are under-taxed, Warren Buffett and President Obama are misleading the American public. In truth, wealthy Americans are already taxed at a higher rate. This is even confirmed by the Congressional Budget Office. The real problem with the federal budget is spending, not taxation.

As we approach the "fiscal cliff" [the fiscal cliff is a popular term for a simultaneous increase in tax rates and decrease in government spending that occurred in January 2013], there was little doubt that famed investor and self-appointed political sage Warren Buffett would pipe in at some point with his periodic call for higher taxes on his ilk of billionaires. Today was the day [November 25, 2012].

Buffett, of course, is welcome to his opinion, but it is amazing that anyone would listen to him on federal budget matters any more than they would listen to Justin Bieber [popular singer] or Jimmy Buffett [popular singer].

Buffett uses the "spaghetti against the wall approach" in his op-ed. In this brand of argument, the writer throws a slew of arguments against the wall to see if anything sticks. Cutting through the plentiful clutter, in essence Buffett argues that we need to raise taxes on the rich to make them write bigger checks to Uncle Sam and thereby lower the deficit. As usual, Buffett's argument for higher taxes falls flat when confronted with basic facts.

Tax Facts

Buffett, the inspiration behind President Obama's much-hyped Buffett Rule, which called for a minimum 30 percent effective tax rate on millionaires, argues again for the same.

The top 1 percent of earners . . . pay an effective tax rate on all federal taxes of 29 percent.

Buffett forgets that we already have a minimum tax. It is called the Alternative Minimum Tax (AMT). And since Congress passed it in the late 1960s, it has become more of a scourge of the middle class than the rich. If Congress foolishly adopted Buffett's minimum tax, we can be sure that it would quickly grow to hammer the middle class the same way the old AMT did.

He also fails to mention that the Buffett Rule is already largely in effect. According to the Congressional Budget Office (CBO), the top 1 percent of earners (those with incomes over $1.2 million in 2009) pay an effective tax rate on all federal taxes of 29 percent. That's almost three times as high as the 11 percent average rate paid by the middle class.

Buffett's argument about the rich paying a lower rate is superficially plausible because the dividend and capital gains tax rates are currently set at 15 percent. Notice that even this rate is greater than the 11 percent average rate applied to the middle class. More critically, this 15 percent rate is applied *after* a 35 percent corporate income tax rate is applied. Buffett, being the world-class investor that he is, of course knows that the corporate tax gets subtracted first. He just ignores that little fact. Maybe somebody will ask him why someday.

That's one half of Buffett's argument debunked with facts.

The Congressional Budget Office

The other half of Buffett's argument is also undone with data from CBO. Buffett writes that we need to raise taxes to get total federal tax revenue up from its current 15.5 percent of GDP [gross domestic product] to 18.5 percent—the historical amount of revenue raised by the federal tax system post–World War II in periods of economic expansion. However, revenues are as low as they are currently because of the slow-growing economy. As the economy recovers, so too will revenues.

Excessive spending is the problem, not low tax revenue.

In 2007, before the worldwide economic meltdown, revenues were at the 18.5 percent of GDP mark. CBO estimates in its "Alternative Fiscal Scenario" that if Congress kept all current tax policies in place—including the Bush-era tax policies and all other tax increases in Taxmageddon (except the payroll tax cut)—tax revenue will surpass 18 percent of GDP in 2016—just four years from now. CBO estimates that revenue will approach 18.5 percent soon thereafter.

The simple fact is that tax increases are not necessary to return tax receipts to their historical level in the near future. All that is needed is for the economy to escape the pall of Obama's economic policies and ignite.

Buffett also calls for spending at about 21 percent of GDP. Currently, the White House estimates that spending will be 24.3 percent of GDP this year—well above Buffett's target. The difference underscores why the fervor to get Republicans to accept tax hikes is so badly misplaced. Excessive spending is the problem, not low tax revenue.

If Buffett still remains worried that tax receipts are too low, despite the facts that show it isn't, he should be reminded that the Treasury Department is happy to take donations from him and his fellow billionaires any time they want to cut a check.

5

The Warren Buffett Rule
Is a Fraud

Patrick Martin

Patrick Martin writes for the World Socialist Web Site, *a forum for socialist ideas and analysis.*

While there has been a great deal of heated discussion over the Buffett Rule, the debate is mostly smoke and mirrors. The Obama administration should tax the wealthy at a higher rate, but it has no intention of doing so. The Buffett Rule, even if instated, would not address the gross inequities between the rich and poor in the United States. Only a very high tax on the rich—which no one is proposing—would start to address these inequities.

If a political fraud could provide millions of jobs, President Obama's demagogic posturing as an advocate of taxing the rich would be the solution to the economic crisis.

Since unveiling his American Jobs Act, followed shortly by a deficit-reduction plan supposedly based on taxing the wealthy, Obama has staged a series of campaign-style appearances to peddle his claim to stand for economic "fairness." At the center of this claim is the so-called Buffett Rule, named after the Omaha billionaire, America's second-wealthiest individual.

Buffett declared in a newspaper column this month [August 2011] that he was paying a lower rate of taxes than his own secretary and condemned the US tax system for "coddling" the super-rich. He has long been one of Obama's biggest contributors, as well as supporting other Democratic Party politicians.

Among a handful of other billionaires, like currency speculator George Soros, Warren Buffett has expressed the concern that the growth of social inequality in the United States, and the transparent bias in tax and budgetary policy in favor of the wealthy, could spark popular discontent and prove destabilizing politically.

Political Posturing

Obama's campaign for the "Buffett Rule" has produced paroxysms of delight on the part of the liberal and middle-class "left" supporters of the administration, including the editorial page of the *New York Times*, columnist Paul Krugman and the *Nation* magazine. A *Times* editorial hailed the tax policy as "sound economics" and a step towards social justice. The *Nation* called for demonstrations to encourage Obama to continue with this supposed shift to the left.

There were equally predictable howls of outrage from the far right. Neoconservative columnist Charles Krauthammer, in a typical screed, declared, "The authentic Obama is a leveler, a committed social democrat, a staunch believer in the redistributionist state, a tribune, above all, of 'fairness'—understood as government-imposed and government-enforced equality."

The hyperventilating on both "left" and right is only part of the political charade in which the Obama campaign seeks to repackage a right-wing, pro–Wall Street administration as the second coming of Franklin Roosevelt. This is part of its effort to delude the American people once again in the 2012 presidential election with the mirage of a "progressive" Democratic Party.

At a rally in Cincinnati Thursday, Obama referred to the charge by Republicans that his tax policy was "class warfare," and declared, "I'm a warrior for the middle class. I'm happy to fight for the middle class. I'm happy to fight for working Americans."

The Buffett Rule is a manifestation of Obama's duplicity.

He followed this up with an appearance Saturday before the annual awards dinner of the Congressional Black Caucus, where he called on his audience to "Take off your bedroom slippers. Put on your marching shoes." As he rebuked those who criticized his administration for favoring the wealthy over the poor and oppressed, the Harvard-educated lawyer dropped his "g's" in a final peroration: "Shake it off. Stop complainin'. Stop grumblin'. Stop cryin'. We are going to press on. We have work to do."

The Buffett Rule's Duplicity

This "work," of course, is the work of serving the vital interests of corporate America at home and American imperialism abroad, from the wars in Iraq, Afghanistan and Libya to the handouts to the banks and giant corporations at the expense of working people.

The Buffett Rule is a manifestation of Obama's duplicity. It is not a rule. The White House has proposed no actual measure to limit tax evasion and tax write-offs by the super-rich, nor will it do so. The "rule" is nothing more than a suggestion to the bipartisan congressional committee tasked with devising at least $1.5 trillion in deficit reduction over the next two months.

Even as a vague suggestion, the Buffett Rule has no chance of being implemented, as Obama knows full well. The six Republican members of the deficit "super-committee" are all committed opponents of any tax increases on the wealthy, while one of the committee Democrats, Senator Max Baucus, was the co-architect of the tax cuts for the wealthy implemented by the [George W.] Bush administration in 2001. Another committee Democrat, Senator John Kerry [appointed secretary of state in 2013], is the wealthiest man in the Senate.

Even if it were to be implemented, the Buffett Rule would not represent the establishment of "fairness" in US taxation. It does not mean a return to the traditional policy of American liberalism in its heyday, when the tax system was used to encourage a very limited redistribution of wealth from the rich to the poor. It merely calls for putting an end to one of the many means by which the US tax system today redistributes wealth in the other direction, from the poor to the rich, by limiting certain tax write-offs enjoyed by billionaires like Buffett.

The Polarization of Wealth

How does establishing an equal rate of taxation for billionaires and secretaries constitute fairness? At the very least, a tax policy based on considerations of fairness and equality would have to address the drastic polarization in wealth and income over the past three decades. During that period, the income gap between the richest 1 percent of Americans and the poorest 40 percent more than tripled, and over the past decade, the wealthy have captured every dollar of increase in national income. Wealth polarization is even greater, with 10 percent of the American population controlling two-thirds of national wealth.

The entire debate over federal tax policy between the Democrats and Republicans is conducted on false premises.

While the Republicans howl about "class warfare," the actual relationship between classes is demonstrated in the steady increase in corporate profits as a share of national income and the corresponding decline in the share of wages. The working class currently receives a smaller proportion of the value that its labor produces than at any time since the period of the Robber Barons.

Federal tax policy has exacerbated this widening social gap. The tax rates on the wealthiest Americans fell from 91 percent in the 1950s and 1960s—under the [Harry S.] Truman, [Dwight D.] Eisenhower and [John F.] Kennedy administrations, hardly bastions of "socialism"—to under 50 percent under [Ronald] Reagan, and now currently at 35 percent. The tax rates on the highest incomes are now at the lowest levels since the early 1920s, before the 1929 Wall Street crash that discredited finance capital for two generations.

Economic life must be freed from the stranglehold of capitalist private ownership.

The entire debate over federal tax policy between the Democrats and Republicans is conducted on false premises. It is not a matter of restoring "fairness," as though such a state of affairs were possible in a society so pervaded by social and economic inequality. What the Socialist Equality Party proposes is a radical redistribution of wealth and income from the rich to the working people—whose labor, after all, is the source of all of society's wealth.

Revamping the Tax Code

We propose, not a tweak in the tax code to remove a few of the most egregious handouts to the super-rich, but a radical and genuinely progressive revamping of tax rates, including a rate of at least 90 percent for all incomes over $500,000, together with a separate wealth tax. Such measures would finance a massive program to put the unemployed to work and rebuild the crumbling social infrastructure of America.

No such reform, however, is possible outside of the mass mobilization of the working class against the corporate-financial elite on the basis of a socialist program. At the center of this program is the nationalization of the corporations and banks and their transformation into publicly owned enterprises under the democratic control of the working population.

Economic life must be freed from the stranglehold of capitalist private ownership of the means of production and reorganized on a genuinely democratic basis to serve the common good, not private profit.

This requires a break by working people from the capitalist two-party system and the building of a mass independent political movement of the working class to fight for a workers' government.

6

Why Taxing the Rich
Is No Solution

Tino Sanandaji and Arvid Malm

Tino Sanandaji is an affiliated researcher at the Institute of Industrial Economics. Arvid Malm is chief economist of the Swedish Taxpayers' Association.

President Obama insists that raising taxes for the rich is only fair. Unfortunately, raising taxes on the rich will only hurt the American economy. If the tax code becomes too oppressive, fewer entrepreneurs would be willing to invest money. It also is an historical fact that each time taxes are raised on the rich, federal tax revenues go down. Instead of raising taxes politicians should close the current tax loopholes.

During the last three decades the wealthy in America have become wealthier yet. American capitalists today are richer than virtually any other group in any country at any point in history. At the same time, the United States is experiencing record deficits, which threaten to bring the economy to its knees.

It is therefore hardly surprising that the solution proposed by some is to raise taxes on the rich. President Obama has proposed doing so. Investing giant Warren Buffett made the case for taxing the wealthy this week in the *New York Times*.

In one respect, Obama and Buffett are completely right. The rich do not "need" to pay lower taxes, and can certainly "afford" tax increases. If raising taxes on the rich would solve the deficit without hurting the economy, we would support the president's tax policy in a heartbeat. It would certainly be a more equitable solution to lower the already astounding standard of living of hedge fund owners than to "cut some kids off from getting a college scholarship."

Unfortunately, the choices faced by America are not that simple. An economic strategy founded on raising taxes on the rich is based on two false premises. The first is that tax increases on the rich are a solution to current budget deficits. The second is the argument often put forward that there is "no evidence" that tax increases on the rich hurt the economy.

If you look carefully, President Obama has never explicitly stated that taxing the rich will bring in much revenue. Instead, the president has made sure to give voters the impression that the Republican refusal to tax the rich is the main cause of the deficit and thus the main obstacle to solving the fiscal crisis. For instance, Obama stated that "tax cuts that went to every millionaire and billionaire in the country" will "force us to borrow an average of $500 billion every year over the next decade." This message has been widely repeated: [Comedy Central host] Jon Stewart, for instance, has assured his impressionable audience that without the [George W.] Bush tax cuts, future deficits would not be a major problem.

Although the proposed tax increases will barely make a dent in the deficit, raising the top tax rates is likely to harm economic output.

But how much revenue are we really talking about? According to the *New York Times*, the president's plan to abolish the Bush tax cuts for those making more than $250,000 is expected to bring in merely $0.7 trillion over the next decade, or about 0.4 percent of Gross Domestic Product [GDP] per year. As a comparison, the Congressional Budget Office estimates that the deficit over the same period is going to be $13 trillion, more than 6 percent of GDP per year.

The rich in America obviously have lots of money, but there are simply not enough of them to fund the president's preferred level of spending. For all the attention it has received, President Obama's "taxing the rich" policy can best be described as symbolic in nature, a rounding error compared to the deficits in the president's budget. Obama centers his speeches around tax hikes on the rich to lead voters into believing that hard choices on the economy can be avoided simply by taxing the rich at a higher rate.

Taxes and Entrepreneurs

Although the proposed tax increases will barely make a dent in the deficit, raising the top tax rates is likely to harm economic output. Many are convinced that tax increases have little or no damaging impact on the economy. We hear over and over again that notions of damaging effects from higher taxes are merely based on "trickle down" theory, which has been proven false.

This is not true. There exists robust empirical evidence that taxes impede economic activity. In conventional economics, only the magnitude of the negative impact of taxes on economic output is debated, not the existence of such an effect.

Let us focus on one such negative impact, the effect of taxes on the activity of business owners, an important segment of the economy. Business owners account for 40 percent of American capital, while firms with less than 500 employees employ half the private sector workforce.

The argument that taxes do not negatively affect small and medium-size business tends to rely on a number of fallacies. One example is an article by Berkeley economics professor Laura Tyson, a member of Obama's advisory board, which was published in the *New York Times*. In the article, she claims that "the relationship between tax rates and economic activity, even though it has superficial appeal, is not supported by the evidence."

The most common fallacy repeated by Tyson is that taxes do not matter because the economy was booming during the Clinton [administration] years even though taxes went up. But tax increases are not the only economic event associated with the Clinton years, and therefore cannot be claimed to cause all events that took place in his presidency. The Clinton years also contained entry into NAFTA [North American Free Trade Agreement], welfare reform, and recovery from the 1992 recession. Most importantly though, the Clinton years included the IT [information technology] boom, which dramatically raised productivity growth in the United States as well as in other developed countries. It would strain the imagination to believe that Clinton's moderate marginal tax increase somehow caused the PC [personal computer] and Internet Revolution.

The Historical Impact of Taxes

Instead of picking one historic event that happens to fit your preferred theory, a more reasonable approach is to investigate all historical periods where taxes increased or decreased. This has been done by former Obama advisor Christina Romer and her husband David Romer. They also take into account the causes of tax increases. They find that tax increases tend to reduce economic growth, stating that "tax increases appear to have a very large, sustained, and highly significant negative impact on output," as "an exogenous tax increase of one percent of GDP lowers real GDP by almost three percent." Similar results have been obtained by Harvard economist Alberto Alesina using a different methodology.

Regarding small business, Tyson claims that "98 percent of small-business owners will not be affected if the Bush tax cuts for these brackets expire." This is true, but also irrelevant. The

United States has more than 25 million registered firms and more than 10 million self-employed. Most registered firms have zero employees and virtually no revenue, and exist for tax or legal reasons. Similarly, most self-employed businesses are small scale and employ no one other than the owner. What we are primarily concerned about is the impact of higher taxes on the small number of economically important firms. These are firms that collect sizable revenue, employ others and have the potential to grow and hire more workers. The owners of such firms are obviously far richer than the typical self-employed person, and are far more likely to be hit by tax increases on higher incomes or on capital gains.

According to the "World Top Incomes Database," 28 percent of the income of the highest earning 1 percent of Americans, the group targeted by the president's tax hikes and the group most likely to own successful firms, is constituted by entrepreneurial income. This has implications for the wider economy. Following the 1986 tax reform, Princeton Professor Harvey Rosen and co-authors investigated the effect of the personal income tax of business owners on their hiring activity. Business owners who received larger tax cuts expanded their hiring more.

While excessive acquisitiveness (greed) is hardly a virtue, acquisitiveness and ambition might not be bad traits in entrepreneurs.

This runs contrary to a common argument that taxes may matter for ordinary people, but not for the already rich or for entrepreneurs who care mainly about developing their company. Arianna Huffington, for example, has ridiculed the notion that the rich would care about and be affected by a few percentage points of higher taxes.

In fact, two groups that are consistently found to be *more* responsive to taxes than average are precisely the self-employed and high-income earners. Both groups can more easily evade taxes and tend to have more control over their economic behavior. Looking at historic American tax reforms, economists Jon Gruber and Emmanuel Saez demonstrate that increases in taxes reduce taxable income especially for high-income earners.

We might like to believe that someone who is already a millionaire doesn't care about obtaining even more money. But this does not appear to be how actual millionaires behave. Even some billionaires actively attempt to lower their tax rates, for example by relocating to tax havens.

While excessive acquisitiveness (greed) is hardly a virtue, acquisitiveness and ambition might not be bad traits in entrepreneurs. Otherwise [Apple founder] Steve Jobs, [Wal-Mart founder] Sam Walton, and [financier] Warren Buffet might have cashed out and retired in Tahiti after making their first $100 million instead of staying on and developing their companies.

While it may offend an egalitarian worldview, top entrepreneurial talent is not easily replaced. "Super-Entrepreneurs" often tend to be extremely talented individuals with access to well-paying, comfortable jobs in already existing firms. In order to entice enough of them to take the risk, hard work, and uncertainty associated with entrepreneurship instead of opting for a safe and well-paying job, there must be a substantial reward associated with success.

One way to better approximate the behavior of innovative entrepreneurs is to study investments in the Venture Capital (VC) sector. VC plays a central role for high-potential firms. More than half of those entrepreneurial firms that were successful enough to make an IPO [initial public offering, where shares of stock are sold to the public] and become public had VC backing. Harvard researchers Josh Lerner and Paul Gompers show that VC fundraising in the United States is highly sensitive to capital gains taxes. Their results indicate that the cause for this is that lower capital gains taxes encourage more skilled individuals to become entrepreneurs.

The low probability of entrepreneurial success even for the talented is often forgotten in the tax debate. Sure, [Bill] Gates and Walton might well still have created Microsoft and Wal-Mart for $25 billion instead of $50 or $100 billion. But for every such success, there are thousands of failures. Entrepreneurship is what economists refer to as a "tournament," a process where many compete for a prize that only a handful will ultimately receive. If taxes reduce the value of the prize, fewer will enter the tournament, even assuming that the behavior of the winners doesn't change. Economists William Gentry and Glenn Hubbard found that high marginal taxes reduce the probability that an individual will enter self-employment to begin with (although admittedly the data did not allow them to establish this definitively).

Another common fallacy in the tax debate is that entrepreneurs do not care about taxes because they are motivated by intrinsic factors. Indeed, non-monetary rewards are important for entrepreneurs (although three-quarters self-report that they also care about monetary rewards). But taxes also matter for the ability to build a new company, even disregarding the personal wealth of the entrepreneur.

Profit taxes lower the amount of capital available for reinvestment. The negative effect of corporate income taxes on business investments has been confirmed by numerous studies, such as a recent one conducted by Harvard economist Andrei Shleifer and co-authors.

Instead of raising tax rates, we can close tax loopholes and broaden the tax base.

Furthermore, the growth of new high-potential ventures depends not only on individual entrepreneurs, but also on the ability to attract talented employees. Like entrepreneurs, these workers often have high paying and rewarding jobs, and a career ladder that they must leave if they choose to work for the new company. Few early stage entrepreneurial firms can compete on wages, instead relying on option programs and promises of future reward. Such incentive mechanisms are made more costly by high taxes, which disproportionally target the small probability of great success.

With higher taxes, even entrepreneurs who do not care about personal gains will find it harder to grow through reinvestment, raising external capital, and attracting new talent. In short, even if you don't care about taxes, taxes care about you.

What to Do About the Tax Code

The United States still leads Western Europe in innovative entrepreneurship. For instance, each year venture capital investments per person are about four to five times higher in the United States than in Western Europe. Is the president willing to risk one of the last sectors in which the United States enjoys a comparative advantage, betting that less burdensome taxes have nothing to do with this competitive edge?

If the tax increases on capitalists proposed by President Obama would balance the budget, perhaps we should endure the damaging effect on economic output. However, as noted above, the impact on the deficit is symbolic in nature. Rather, the motivation appears to be political, a combination of resentment towards the rich and a reaction to excessively ideological supply-siders.

Currently, less than half of national income is included in the basis for taxable income. Instead of raising tax rates, we can close tax loopholes and broaden the tax base so as to raise revenue to its historic average, while controlling federal spending. This is preferable to increasing tax rates based on the faulty notion that raising taxes on the rich does not hurt economic output.

7

Rich Americans Are Not Over-Taxed

Sarah Ayres and Michael Linden

Sarah Ayres is a research associate with the Economic Policy team at the Center for American Progress. Michael Linden is director of tax and budget policy at the Center for American Progress.

The debate over whether wealthy Americans should pay more taxes has been skewed by conservatives. Much of the presented information, stating that rich Americans are already over-taxed, is misleading. In truth, the rich pay fewer taxes than they did thirty years ago. This has left more of a burden on the middle class, leading to a widening divide between the rich and poor. If the rich pay more taxes than the poor percentage-wise, there is a simple explanation: The rich have more money to tax.

Rich Americans are not overtaxed. Not by a long shot. From 1996 to 2007 the overall federal tax rate for the richest 1 percent fell by more than 6 percentage points. The top marginal income tax rate dropped from 70 percent in 1980 to 35 percent today. And that's just for starters.

The [George W.] Bush tax cuts, enacted in 2001 and 2003, delivered massive new tax breaks to the rich, reducing a millionaire's tax bill by hundreds of thousands of dollars. And tax benefits—such as the home mortgage interest deduction, the charitable deduction, and the employer provided health care exclusion—all benefit the rich more than they benefit the middle class. One in four millionaires pays a lower overall tax rate than millions of middle-class families.

Not surprisingly, then—given the enormous federal budget challenges we are currently facing—many people have come to the reasonable conclusion that the rich can and should be asked to pay a little more. But raising taxes on the richest 1 percent, even slightly, is anathema to the modern-day conservative movement. And since their argument that cutting taxes for rich people is economically good for everyone only goes so far these days—remember how the Bush tax cuts turned out—they have turned to a different bogus argument: The rich already pay more than their fair share.

Misleading Information

How can conservatives possibly argue that the rich are over-taxed given all the evidence and facts to the contrary? They rely on one totally misleading statistic: share of overall taxes paid. Here's the familiar conservative litany on the subject:

- Rep. Michele Bachmann (R-MN): "The top 1 percent of income-earners pay about 40 percent of all taxes to the federal government."

- Former President George W. Bush advisor Karl Rove: "One percent of American taxpayers pay 39 percent of the burden."

- Speaker of the House John Boehner: "Come on. The top 1 percent pay 38 percent of the income taxes in America. You know, how much more do you want them to pay?"

- Rep. Larry Buschon (R-IN): "Arguing right now that the higher income earners aren't paying their fair share is not true. . . . the top 1 percent of income earners are paying about 38 percent of the taxes."

And you can find the same basic statistic being cited by the Heritage Foundation, the Tax Foundation, and the Cato Institute.

One percent of the people paying 40 percent of all the taxes? It sounds unfair, right? But stop to think about it for more than a moment and it becomes apparent that the statistic is meaningless.

First of all, federal income taxes are only one part of the overall tax system. By focusing only on the one piece of the tax code that is very progressive, conservatives are artificially inflating the share of taxes paid by the 1 percent.

Second, the rich pay most of the taxes because they make most of the income. Think about it: Of course the richest 1 percent of people pay way more than 1 percent of all the taxes—they have way more than 1 percent of all the income. That's why they are in the top 1 percent.

Payroll taxes, which make up 40 percent of all federal revenue, are regressive.

Third, the share of taxes paid is a really silly way to think about tax burden. What matters isn't the amount of taxes someone pays as a share of total revenues. What matters is the amount of taxes someone pays as a share of his or her own income.

The Total Tax Burden

When Rep. Bachmann or Karl Rove or anyone else claims that 1 percent of Americans pay 40 percent of all taxes, they are flat out wrong. That's because they are conflating the federal income tax with all taxes. It's true that in 2007 (the last year for which complete data are available) the richest 1 percent paid about 40 percent of all the federal income taxes. But the federal income tax is only one part of the federal tax system, and of course, there are also state and local taxes.

In fact, federal income taxes make up just 42 percent of all federal taxes, and only one-quarter of all taxes, systemwide across our country. The federal income tax is progressive—meaning that higher-income households pay, on average, higher tax rates—but it's practically the only piece of our country's tax system that is.

Payroll taxes, which make up 40 percent of all federal revenue, are regressive. According to the nonpartisan Congressional Budget Office, or CBO, in 2007 a household in the middle class paid about 9.5 percent of their income in payroll taxes while someone in the top 1 percent paid just 1.6 percent of their income in payroll taxes. State and local taxes are also regressive. The Institute for Taxation and Economic Policy reported that the average state and local effective tax rate for the top 1 percent is only 5.2 percent, while the average tax rate on the middle 20 percent is 9.4 percent.

By ignoring the regressive parts of federal, state, and local tax codes, and either implicitly or explicitly suggesting that federal income taxes are the only taxes, conservatives are artificially inflating the share of taxes paid by the rich. When other federal and nonfederal taxes are taken into account, the 1 percent's share of taxes paid declines quite a lot.

The CBO found that the top 1 percent paid 28.1 percent of the total federal tax burden in 2007. And a more recent analysis by the Tax Policy Center estimates that the share of federal taxes paid by the top 1 percent dropped to 25.6 percent in 2011.

Furthermore, the share of taxes paid by the top 1 percent drops even more when taking into account state and local taxes. An analysis by Citizens for Tax Justice found that when state and local taxes are included the share of total taxes paid by the top 1 percent in 2010 is only 21.5 percent. This is just about half the "headline" 40 percent that conservatives like to claim.

The Rich Make More Income

Still, the richest 1 percent do pay much more than 1 percent of all the taxes. But, of course, that's because they take home much more than 1 percent of all the income. In fact, the share of total taxes paid by the top 1 percent is almost identical to the share of total income going to the top 1 percent. In 2010 the richest 1 percent took home 20.3 percent of all income, and—as noted above—paid 21.5 percent of all the taxes.

The share of taxes paid by the rich matches up pretty closely to the share of income they make.

Furthermore, the share of federal taxes paid by the rich increased at almost exactly the same rate as their share of income increased. Conservatives often point out that the top 1 percent's share of taxes increased over the past few decades as evidence that the rich are taxed too much. In a report on income inequality, for example, House Budget Committee Chairman Paul Ryan (R-WI) lamented that "the share of the federal tax burden borne by the top 1 percent increased dramatically."

Yes, the share of federal taxes paid by the top 1 percent of income earners has increased from 14.2 percent in 1980 to 28.1 percent in 2007. But at the same time, the top 1 percent's share of total income has more than doubled. In other words, the richest Americans are paying more of the taxes now than they were in 1980 because they are now making that much more of the nation's income. The rising share of taxes paid by the top 1 percent in the past three decades is not evidence that the rich are now overtaxed; it's evidence of rising inequality.

Don't Forget About Wealth

So the share of taxes paid by the rich matches up pretty closely to the share of income they make. But relative to their share of wealth, the richest 1 percent are actually making out like bandits. Wealth is an important measurement to consider in addition to income because it helps to paint a more complete picture of someone's ability to pay.

To put in perspective the difference between income and wealth, consider that to be in the top 1 percent of income earners, a household needs an adjusted gross income of at least $380,000, or 11 times the median household adjusted gross income of $33,000. But to be in the top 1 percent of wealthy Americans, a household needs a net worth of almost $14 million—225 times that of the median family net worth of just $62,000 in 2009. And the richest 1 percent of Americans own an even greater share of wealth than of income. Economists estimate that the wealthiest 1 percent own between 35 percent and 40 percent of the nation's entire wealth.

An Irrelevant Measurement

Given the fact that the share of taxes paid by the rich is in near perfect proportion to the share of income garnered by the rich, and is actually very low compared to the share of the wealth owned by the rich, it should be fairly clear at this point that "share of taxes paid" is a not a particularly useful measurement of tax fairness or tax burden.

Share of taxes paid means nothing to individual taxpayers and says nothing about the overall tax system. No taxpayer has ever said: "Wow, my share of federal taxes this year was 0.00000041 percent instead of the 0.00000040 percent it was last year!" But that same taxpayer will care quite a lot if the amount of taxes he pays as a share of his own income goes up.

The share of taxes paid is also useless as a measure of fairness. Consider, for example, a hypothetical village of 100 people. In this village, there is one rich man who makes $1,000 a year and 99 other villagers who each make $10 a year. Now imagine that everyone in this village pays exactly the same overall tax rate of 10 percent. The one man who makes

$1,000—the richest 1 percent of the village—will end up paying more than 50 percent of all the taxes. Is that unfair? Of course not. He's making more than 50 percent of all the income, and everyone is paying exactly the same tax rate.

Or consider this: What if the rich man in the village actually paid a lower effective tax rate than the rest of the villagers—say 5 percent? Then his share of taxes paid would still be more than 33 percent. In that case, the tax code is actually regressive, asking the 99 poorer people to pay more of their income in taxes than the one rich man does. And yet if you looked only at *share of taxes paid*, you might be led to believe otherwise.

The rich pay more because they have more, period.

The fact that a tax system can be regressive and still result in the rich paying the biggest share of taxes is a good indicator that share of taxes paid is not a measure of tax fairness.

A Bogus Argument

If you hear the words "share of taxes paid" used in conjunction with an argument for why the rich already pay too much in taxes, then you can be pretty sure that the argument doesn't hold water. Share of taxes paid is a misleading and fundamentally unreliable statistic that reveals little, if anything, about the fairness or relative burden of the tax system.

The truth is that the richest 1 percent only pay about 20 percent of the total taxes, which is just about equal to their share of the nation's income and only about half their share of the nation's wealth. The rise in the share of federal taxes paid by the richest 1 percent can be explained entirely by their increasing share of national income—the two numbers have moved in near perfect harmony for the past 30 years.

Finally, and most importantly, the relationship between actual progressivity in the tax code and share of taxes paid is tenuous at best. The distribution of taxes paid is far more related to the underlying distribution of income than it is to the real measure of progressivity: effective tax rates.

It may sound unfair, at first blush, that 1 percent of Americans pay much more than 1 percent of all the taxes. But share of taxes paid is a statistic designed to cloud the issue, not clarify it. The rich pay more because they have more, period. What is truly unfair is that some in the 1 percent can use special rates, loopholes, and tax benefits to reduce their tax bill so much that they end up paying a lower share of their income in taxes than average working families. That is the real unfairness in the tax code.

8

Taxing the Rich Will Improve the US Economy

Dave Johnson

Dave Johnson is a fellow with the Campaign for America's Future and a senior fellow with Renew California.

Many of the economic and social problems of today could be fixed by returning to higher tax rates for the wealthy. All this would require would be returning to the structure of the tax code during the 1950s. Then, the tax rate for the wealthy was 90 percent. This offered a number of built-in economic protections and provided more government revenue. By returning to this code, the United States also could return to the so-called happier days of the 1950s.

A return to [Dwight D.] Eisenhower-era 90% top tax rates helps fix our economy in several ways:

1. It makes it take longer to end up with a fortune. In fact it makes people *build* and *earn* a fortune, instead of shooting for quick windfalls. This forces long-term thinking and planning instead of short-term scheming and scamming. If grabbing everything in sight and running doesn't pay off anymore, you have to change your strategy.

2. It gets rid of the quick-buck-scheme business model. Making people take a longer-term approach to building rather than grabbing a fortune will help reattach businesses to communities by reinforcing interdependence between businesses

and their surrounding communities. When it takes owners and executives years to build up a fortune they need *solid companies that are around for a long time.* This requires the surrounding public infrastructure of roads, schools, police, fire, courts, etc., to be in good shape to provide *long-term support for the enterprise.* You also want your company to build a solid reputation for serving its customers rather than cheapening the product, pursuing quick-buck scams, cutting customer service, etc. The current Wall Street/private equity business model of looting companies, leaving behind an empty shell, unemployed workers and a surrounding community in devastation will no longer be a viable business strategy.

3. It will lower the executive crime rate. Today it is possible to run scams that let you pocket huge sums in a single year, and leave behind the mess you make for others to fix. A high top tax rate removes the incentive to lie, cheat and steal to grab every buck you can as fast as you can. This reduces the temptation to be dishonest. If you aren't going to keep the whole dime, why risk doing the time? When excessive, massive paydays are possible, it opens the door to overwhelming greed and a resulting compromising of principles. Sort of the definition of the decades since [Ronald] Reagan, no?

4. Combined with badly needed cuts in military spending—we spend more on military than all other countries on earth *combined*—taxing the wealthy ends budget deficits and starts paying off the massive Reagan/[George H.W.] Bush debt. This reduces and ultimately eliminates the share of the budget that goes to pay interest. The United States now has to pay a huge share of its budget just to cover the interest on the borrowing that tax cuts made necessary. Paying off the debt would remove this huge drag on our economy. (Never mind that [economist] Alan Greenspan famously called for [George W.] Bush's tax cuts by saying it was dangerous to pay off our debt—now that same Alan Greenspan says we need to cut benefits to retired people because our debt is so high.)

5. It will bring in revenue to pay for improvements in infrastructure that then cause the economy to explode for the better. Investing in modern transit systems, smart grid, energy efficiency, fast internet and other improvements leads to a huge payoff of increased prosperity for all of us—especially for those at the top income levels. Infrastructure improvement and maintenance is the "seed corn" of economic growth. We have been eating that seed corn since Reagan's tax cuts.

A look at economic growth rate charts shows a steady decline in the decades since top tax rates began to fall.

---

6. (related) It will bring in revenue for improving our schools, colleges and universities. Not only will this help our competitiveness, but it will improve each of our lives and level of happiness.

7. It will boost economic growth and rebuild a strong middle class. A consumption-based economy does better when consumers have more to spend. Perhaps not cause-and-effect, though I suspect so, but after FDR [President Franklin D. Roosevelt] raised top tax rates the economy grew dramatically. The 90% top rate years under FDR, [Harry] Truman, Eisenhower and the beginning of the [John F.] Kennedy years were the years when we built the middle class. And remember, after [Bill] Clinton raised top tax rates only modestly the economy grew. How's it been doing since [George W.] Bush's tax cuts for the rich?

A look at economic growth rate charts shows a steady decline in the decades since top tax rates began to fall. Is it just a coincidence that the economy booms after tax increases that provide revenue to invest in new "seed corn," and that the economy declines as we reduce taxes?

8. It is good for business because increased revenue will enable increasing government spending for the benefit of regular people. This recirculates money into the economy

more productively than the current system of putting huge fortunes into a few hands and hoping for a resulting consumption of high-end goods. The wealthy can only spend so much, so more disposable income in the hands of regular people is good for business. Any business owner will tell you they want customers more than they want tax cuts. (Let's wait until the top one percent no longer owns most of everything before we talk about whether there is an effect on investment.)

9. It protects working people. Exploiting workers with long hours, low pay or lack of pay increases, lack of worker protections, firing union organizers and schemes that call employees "contractors" will no longer pay off as it does today. The era of extreme union-busting came in at the same time as the tax cuts. . . .

10. It redistributes income and wealth in ways that help all of us. Currently a few people receive most of the income and own most of everything. A very high top tax rate reduces this concentration of wealth.

11. It fights the political instability that results from concentration of wealth. Great inequality in a society and the resulting loss of opportunity results in political instability that can lead to extreme ideologies, rebellion, etc. We are seeing all the signs of a resurgence of these problems today.

12. It will help rebuild our sense of democracy and belief in equality. As we have seen and are seeing, when too much is in the hands of too few, they have too much power and influence and use it to get even more.

13. It will strengthen the government that *We, the People* have worked hard to build, and strengthen its ability to enforce the laws and regulations that protect all of us and the resources we hold in common. It will increase its ability to provide all of us *equally* with the benefits of our joint efforts and our economy.

14. Finally, for good measure, increasing top tax rates will cause those affected to work harder to make up the difference.

The Ayn Randians [related to libertarian writer Ayn Rand] claim the very rich are the "producers" and all the rest of us are just parasites and slackers who feed off their "work." So it will be very good for our economy to get them working harder by taxing them at 90%! You may have heard about those 25 hedge fund managers who brought in *an average of $1 billion each* last year—an amount that would have paid for 658,000 teachers—while the rest of the country suffered through a terrible economy. If we had a top tax rate of 90% they would "only" take home $100 million or so each—in a single year. And we could have 658,000 more teachers. So it's a win-win.

Taxes are how we all pitch in to enjoy the benefits and protections of modern society. Those benefits and protections are what enable people to become wealthy, and we ask that they give some back so others can prosper as well.

9

Taxing the Rich Will Not Improve the US Economy

Michael Medved

Michael Medved is a talk show host, film critic, and political commentator.

While a number of commentators are claiming that the tax code of the 1950s worked better, the truth is more complicated. Higher rates on wealthy Americans have always led to lower revenues for the federal government. As a result, the government has less money to spend on social projects. In looking for an easy way to fix the American economy, many have succumbed to nostalgia stripped of the harder truths.

Americans have always reveled in nostalgia about the music, fashion or favorite foods of bygone eras, but a sudden yearning for the high tax rates of yesteryear seems new and strange. While some opinion leaders pine openly for the tax system that once claimed a big majority of income from top earners, their cozy, communitarian vision offers a deeply distorted view of those good old days.

In his defiant "Twinkie Manifesto," professor Paul Krugman, Nobel Prize winner in economics, affectionately cites "the '50s—the Twinkie Era" for "lessons that remain relevant in the 21st century." He particularly applauds the fact that "incomes in the top brackets faced a marginal tax rate of 91%," and later 70% in the 1960s. He associates that policy with "spectacular, widely shared economic growth: Nothing before or since has matched the doubling of median family income between 1947 and 1973."

Higher rates on a few wealthy taxpayers didn't produce higher revenues.

A group called New Hampshire Labor News, self-described "union members and advocates," similarly praised the golden year of 1952 on the *Daily Kos*, featuring the headline "Tax Policy: Time to Go Back to the Future?" At *The Huffington Post*, Dave Johnson has been pushing old-time tax rates for years, including an earnest offering entitled "14 Ways a 90% Top Tax Rate Fixes Our Economy." Meanwhile, Krugman's fellow *New York Times* columnist Nicholas Kristof recently caught the fever to punish the rich with grandpa's tax rates because "half-a-century of tax cuts focused on the wealthiest Americans leave us with third-rate public services."

As Congress careens toward the dreaded "fiscal cliff," I've also been deluged by callers to my radio show who wistfully recall the higher top taxes of the Nifty Fifties as an instant cure for the current crisis.

Higher Rates, Lower Revenues

The problem with this odd wave of high tax nostalgia is that it ignores one crucial fact about the [Dwight D.] Eisenhower era: Higher rates on a few wealthy taxpayers didn't produce higher revenues. Official figures show that at the end of the Eisenhower administration (1958–60), tax payments to government at all levels averaged 28% of the gross domestic product [GDP]. Today, that number tops 32%.

Even separating federal taxes from local and state taxes, the government in Washington alone takes a bigger bite out of the national paycheck than it did in the warmly remembered *Leave It to Beaver* era. In the years 1950–59, annual direct revenues to the feds averaged 17.2% of GDP; in the comparable period of the Bush-Obama era (2000–09), even with tax cuts and economic collapse, that figure was 17.7% of GDP.

How could the federal government grab a bigger share of national income when top marginal rates had fallen by nearly two-thirds from their high point under Ike [President Eisenhower]?

Those who express their fervent longing to return to the days of 90% tax rates would never welcome the lower levels of revenue or spending that went along with them.

For one thing, the theoretical top rates applied to almost no one—with estimates that only 0.01% of 1960s taxpayers officially qualified to pay Uncle Sam at the highest level. Indeed, today's richest 5% cover a much bigger share of the total tax burden than the old rich ever did. In the good old days of 70% top rates, rich taxpayers covered barely a third of the 60% share of income taxes that they pay today.

Government Spending

The oddest aspect of the nostalgia for high taxes involves the failure to consider the other half of any fiscal equation: The levels of government spending. Krugman, Kristof and kindred strongly suggest that lower tax rates lead inexorably toward reduced levels of government services and public sector investments. But the numbers tell a different story.

In 1956, the year of Ike's landslide re-election, the federal government's outlays came to 16.5% of GDP; this year, Uncle Sam is spending an unprecedented 24.3%, the second highest figure in the 66 years since World War II. While leading lights of the left complain (with justification) about greater inequality and reduced social mobility, they can't blame those problems on lower government spending. Washington pays out more than ever in every major arena other than defense. Countless expensive programs (Medicare, Medicaid, ObamaCare) have been launched since the '50s without replicating that epoch's admirable growth.

Those who express their fervent longing to return to the days of 90% tax rates would never welcome the lower levels of revenue or spending that went along with them. Like most dreamers who wallow in nostalgia, they obsess on one cherished element of the past without acknowledging the inconvenient truths that surrounded it.

10

Taxing the Rich Will Not Pay Off the US Deficit

David Brown, Gabe Horwitz, and David Kendall

David Brown is a policy advisor for Third Way's Economic Program. Gabe Horwitz directs Third Way's Economic Program. David Kendall is a senior fellow for Health and Fiscal Policy.

When multiple tax scenarios are considered, raising the taxes on the wealthy will not totally resolve the current federal budget crisis. At the heart of the crisis is the growing cost of entitlements. To maintain these entitlements, taxes need to be raised on wealthy and middle-class Americans. Unfortunately, most of the solutions offered fail to consider the long-term impact of entitlements.

In order to demonstrate that taxes alone cannot solve our budget woes, we explore three budget scenarios, all of which rely solely on revenue and leave entitlements and other spending as is.

- *Scenario I* includes each of the Democrats' key proposals for taxing the wealthy: roll back the [George W.] Bush tax cuts for those with high incomes, limit their deductions, bump up the estate tax, and pass the Buffett Rule. *Even if each major Democratic* *proposal to raise taxes on the wealthy becomes law, the national debt will double as a share of the economy by 2035, and the annual deficit in 2040 will exceed $4 trillion, in inflation-adjusted dollars.*

- *Scenario II* piles on more tax hikes for the rich, enough for the government to reach and surpass its record-high level for revenue as a percentage of GDP [gross domestic product] (averaging 21% of GDP between 2014 and 2040). In this second scenario we aim all of the tax hikes on the wealthy with only a smattering hitting the near-wealthy. *Even with tax rates for the wealthy at 50%—higher than any rates under discussion—the national debt will double as a share of the economy by 2040, and the annual deficit that year will exceed $3 trillion, in inflation-adjusted dollars.*

- *Scenario III* shows the volume of tax hikes needed for taxes to single-handedly contain long-term deficits. This scenario keeps the tax hikes on the wealthy from Scenario I, leaves entitlements on autopilot, and pushes deficits to the target level with additional tax increases on everyone. *Relying on taxes alone to hold long-term deficits at 3% of GDP would require phasing in a 60% tax increase on the median-income family, raising its annual tax burden by $6,200, in 2012 dollars.*

As we have noted previously, entitlements provide critical economic security. But unless taxes rise dramatically, status-quo entitlements will prevent government from doing much else. An all-of-the-above approach on the budget is the only way to preserve entitlements, make room for needed public investments, and spare the middle class from tough tax hikes in the future.

Roll Back the Bush Tax Cuts

Starting in 2013:

- Raise the top two tax rates, on ordinary income over $250,000 a year for joint filers, to [Bill] Clinton [era] levels (39.6% and 36%).

- Raise the top capital gains rate by 5 percentage points (to 23.8%).

- Tax qualified dividends as ordinary income.

- Reduce the value of exemptions and deductions for wealthy taxpayers.

- Restore the estate tax to its 2009 level: a top rate of 45% and exclusion of $3.5 million.

- Impose the Buffett Rule, requiring all earners of over $1 million to pay at least 30% in taxes.

Scenario I shows the long-term budgetary effects of the revenue increases on high-income earners proposed in the President's 2013 budget. The top two tax rates, on ordinary income over $250,000 for married couples (over $200,000 for individuals), are returned to Clinton-era levels. The estate tax is restored to its 2009 level. Rules limiting the value of personal exemptions and itemized deductions for the wealthy are reinstated. Plus, a cap is imposed on the value of tax preferences claimed by the wealthy. And to make sure millionaires pay at least a 30% effective tax rate, the Buffett Rule kicks in. These proposals protect the middle class from tax hikes entirely and would increase revenue by roughly $1.6 trillion over ten years.

This revenue would temporarily drop annual deficits close to the 3% target that economists deem preferable. But in the next decade:

- Entitlement costs skyrocket and revenue can't keep up.

- Federal borrowing is so prolific that interest payments consume an unprecedented share of the economy.

- Annual deficits will be $800 billion in 2020, $2.5 trillion in 2030, and $4.2 trillion in 2040—all in today's dollars.

- *Even if each major Democratic proposal to raise taxes on the wealthy becomes law, the national debt will double as a share of the economy by 2035.*

The end of Bush tax cuts for the wealthy should be part of a deficit grand bargain but cannot be its mainstay. With deficit growth similar to that under Scenario I, a U.S. fiscal crisis would be increasingly likely. Investors would eventually demand higher interest rates for U.S. Treasuries, driving up the cost of government borrowing. As Europe has recently shown, that sequence can unfold rapidly, forcing spending cuts and tax increases much more drastic than if they had come sooner.

Soak the Rich

Starting in 2013:

- All Scenario I tax increases, plus . . .

- Raise the top ordinary income rate, on income over $388,350 for joint filers, by 10 additional percentage points (from 39.6% to 49.6%).

- Raise the second and third-highest ordinary income rates, on income between $217,450 and $388,350, by 5 additional percentage points (from 33% and 36% to 38% and 41%).

- Raise the rates on capital gains by 15 percentage points each (from 10% and 23.8% to 25% and 38.8%).

- Increase the cap for the Social Security payroll tax, from $107,000 to $170,000, and adjust for wage growth.

If ending Bush tax cuts for the wealthy is insufficient, can additional taxes on the wealthy solve long-term deficits?

Scenario II looks out over 30 years and sets average federal revenue over that period to 21% of GDP—a level achieved only once (during World War II). We add to Scenario I by lifting the top ordinary income rates to levels beyond those under President Clinton or in President Obama's proposals. For joint filers, taxes on income over $388,350 increase from 35% today to 49.6%. Income between $217,450 and $388,350, subject to one 33% rate today, would face two brackets of 38% and 41%. The Social Security payroll tax cap jumps from $107,000 to $170,000 and rises with wage growth. Capital gains rates climb 15 percentage points above Scenario I, reaching 38.8% for wealthy filers and 25% for the rest.

These measures all target the wealthy and near-wealthy and would collect $3.5 trillion over ten years. Revenue as a percentage of GDP would rise from 19.1% in 2014 to 22.7% in 2040, averaging 21% of GDP over that period.

Very high taxes on the wealthy will only go so far.

Tax rates this high would achieve healthy deficit levels through the decade but not beyond. This revenue boost still isn't close to matching the entitlement surge coming in the next decade.

- By not controlling entitlement spending, interest payments continue to fuel rising deficits.

- Annual deficits will be $500 billion in 2020, $2.0 trillion in 2030, and $3.3 trillion in 2040—all in today's dollars.

- *Even with tax rates for the wealthy at 50%—higher than any rates under discussion—the national debt will double as a share of the economy by 2040.*

Whether or not this scenario is politically possible (given the high tax rates) the point is clear: very high taxes on the wealthy will only go so far. Deficits would still grow large enough to threaten a fiscal crisis. To achieve long-term budget security and leave entitlements on auto-pilot, a revenue-only approach would require tax increases on the middle class, as is shown in Scenario III.

A Middle Class Tax Hike

- Keep deficits at or below 3% of GDP from 2017 to 2040.

- Maintain current path of entitlement spending.

- Starting in 2013: All Scenario I tax increases.

- Starting in 2015: Increase the cap for the Social Security payroll tax, to $170,000 (Scenario II). Increase the payroll tax rate for Medicare by 1 percentage point (to 3.9%).

- Starting in 2019: Increase all tax rates on ordinary income 5 additional percentage points, phased in over 10 years. Increase both tax rates on capital gains 10 percentage points (to 20% and 33.8%), phased in over 5 years.

- Starting in 2023: Impose a 10% national value-added tax, phased in over 5 years.

For taxes alone to keep deficits sustainable and leave entitlement spending untouched, revenue in 2040 must reach

27% of GDP, well above the World War II record of 21%. To achieve that, middle class tax hikes are unavoidable.

Scenario III shows the magnitude of tax increases needed if Congress decides to contain deficits by 2017 and ignore entitlement spending. The President's proposed revenue increases, from Scenario I, are enough to push deficits below 4% of GDP by 2015. To push them to 3%, Congress could elect to raise revenue within two programs threatening the deficit, Social Security and Medicare. Raising the cap on the Social Security payroll tax (Scenario I) and raising the Medicare payroll tax 1 percentage point would keep deficits below 3% in 2017 and 2018.

Then, with fast-rising entitlement costs looming, Congress would be forced to raise revenue substantially. Reasonable tax increases on the wealthy alone, already employed through the President's existing proposals, simply can't raise enough money. So in 2019, Congress turns to the most powerful tool at its disposal: rate increases across the board. Each ordinary income rate gradually rises by 5 percentage points, and each capital gains rate gradually rises by 10 percentage points.

The above tax increases contain deficits only through 2022, when entitlement spending is still accelerating. In need of revenue typical of European governments, Congress turns to a European-style tax still unused by the United States. In 2023, Congress begins phasing in a 10-percent national value-added tax (VAT). A popular tax reform idea among economists, the VAT is also regressive, so many existing VAT proposals return significant proceeds to lower and middle-income taxpayers. But in Scenario III, the 10% rate collects just enough revenue to meet the government's obligations; a considerable rebate would require a much higher rate.

Because of its broad sweep, Scenario III delivers enough revenue to stabilize the debt. As federal spending rises, federal revenue keeps pace. Lower interest payments help contain federal spending, and debt—as a share of the economy—begins a slow decline.

But to do this, Scenario III hits middle class families hard—and that is only if taxes on the wealthy reach levels beyond what the President currently proposes. For example, the median income of jointly filing couples is $76,561. A family of that income level, which has two children and claims the standard deduction, pays a total of $10,406 in federal taxes. *Relying on taxes alone to hold long-term deficits at 3% of GDP would require phasing in a 60% tax increase on the median-income family, raising its annual tax burden by $6,200, in 2012 dollars.*

Significant revenue must be part of the solution, but fiscal responsibility cannot ignore entitlements.

Under Scenario III, that tax increase on the median-income family would consist of:

- Higher income tax rates: $2,473

- Higher payroll tax rate: $383

- Burden of national value-added tax (through higher prices): $3,341

Scenario III is our projection of what an all-revenue budget fix would look like, but there are numerous other ways to reach the target through taxes. However, it's hard to keep the middle class from harm. For example, acclaimed economist Simon Johnson and coauthor James Kwak advocate only minor changes to entitlement programs but call for numerous tax increases, many of which fall directly on the middle class. Their plan increases the rates of the Social Security payroll tax, the Medicare payroll tax, the gas tax, and the capital gains tax. It slashes a big middle class deduction and exemption, for mortgage interest and employer-sponsored health insurance. It also adds a new carbon tax and value-added tax.

Whether you're looking at Scenario III or other serious proposals, one thing is certain: fixing long-term deficits without touching entitlements may be possible in theory, but would punish the middle class with higher taxes.

Meeting Tomorrow's Priorities

Entitlement programs provide critical economic security to the elderly and the vulnerable. Investments provide opportunities for the economy to grow and for individuals to achieve personal economic success. The tax code must deliver sufficient revenue to support both of these pillars, allowing the government to keep running while allowing people to save, invest, and consume. In today's budget, none of these priorities are where they should be, and in tomorrow's budget the situation only worsens.

Significant revenue must be part of the solution, but fiscal responsibility cannot ignore entitlements. The fastest growing part of our budget is driven by entitlements, and these programs must take their share of reductions in a reasoned way to protect the elderly and the vulnerable.

The fiscal cliff presents a once-in-a-generation moment. Government leaders have an opportunity to create a balanced plan that gives us the economic certainty we need for growth and prosperity for decades to come.

11

Low Tax Rates for the Wealthy Have Widened the Gap Between Rich and Poor

Andre Damon

Andre Damon writes for the World Socialist Web Site.

Between 1992 and 2007, the richest Americans grew richer. At the same time, these wealthy Americans paid fewer taxes. This was true during the administrations of both Bill Clinton and George W. Bush. The end result of these tax policies has been to create a greater divide between the rich and the poor.

The incomes of the very rich in the US grew phenomenally between 1992 and 2007, while their tax rates plummeted, according to recently uncovered IRS [Internal Revenue Service] statistics.

The figures were published on the IRS web site in December of 2009, but received little notice because they were not announced. The report only became widely known when Tax Analysts, a news outlet for tax information, discovered the document and wrote about it on its web site, tax.com, on Thursday [February 18, 2010].

The report shows that the average income for the top-earning 400 families, denominated in 1990 dollars, grew from $17 million to $87 million, representing a five-fold increase in real terms. During this time, the percentage of the total national income that went to the top 400 families tripled, from .52 percent in 1992 to 1.59 in 2007.

The data shows that these families saw their incomes increase by 31 percent between 2006 and 2007 alone, while the average income of each family reached $345 million.

The amount of money earned by the group more than doubled from 2001, when its members earned on average $131.1 million. In 1993, the top 400 tax return filings amounted on average to $46 million. This means that there was an eight-fold nominal increase in the average earnings for this group between 1993 and 2007.

Lower Taxes for the Wealthy

Meanwhile, the effective tax rate on this group—the amount actually paid in taxes—fell to 16.6 percent, the lowest figure on IRS records dating to 1992.

Congressional Democrats have sought to place blame for falling taxes on the wealthy solely on the [George W.] Bush administration's tax cuts. But the IRS figures show that the effective tax rate on the top 400 income earners actually fell faster under the last part of the Clinton administration than at any later time.

The effective tax rate hit a high point of nearly 29 percent in 1995. By the end of the Clinton administration, the rate had fallen to 22 percent. The trend continued under Bush, with the effective tax rate falling another 6 percentage points between 2001 and 2007.

If the top 400 earners had been taxed in 2007 at the 1995 rate, they would have paid an additional $18.4 billion in taxes.

The Bush administration lowered the capital gains tax by 5 percentage points, to 15 percent, in 2003. But Bush's policies were only a continuation of laws passed under the Clinton administration, when the capital gains tax was lowered from 28 percent to 20 percent for the top income brackets.

The top income earners received a total income of $138 billion in 2007. This figure is larger than the yearly output of most of the world's countries, and is nearly as large as the GDP [gross domestic product] of Chile. Out of this amount, the group paid only $23 billion in taxes.

If the top 400 earners had been taxed in 2007 at the 1995 rate, they would have paid an additional $18.4 billion in taxes, enough to cover the entire 2010 budget shortfall of the state of California.

About three quarters of income for earners in this tax bracket came from capital gains, which were taxed at 15 percent, as opposed to income, which is taxed at a rate of 35 percent for the top bracket.

The top 400 families actually paid lower taxes compared to other high-income earners. In 2005, the Congressional Budget Office found that the top 1 percent as a whole paid a tax rate of 19.7 percent.

The median 20 percent of income earners paid a tax rate of 12.5 percent, including Social Security payments, which are negligible for the very rich.

It is the rich who have bankrupted the state, with the full assistance of the two big-business parties.

The IRS report on the top 400 families was first regularly published by the Clinton administration, but the Bush administration shut down its release, according to the tax.com article by [David] Cay Johnston, a tax law professor at Syracuse University. The Obama administration resumed publication of the figures, with the 2006 figures published about a year ago.

Johnston also noted, "At least three hedge fund managers made $3 billion in 2007." He added, "Only 33 of the top 400 paid an effective tax rate of 30 percent to 35 percent, which is the maximum federal tax rate."

A Growing Divide

The data further substantiates the highly publicized conclusions of economists Thomas Piketty and Emmanuel Saez, who found that two thirds of income increases between 2002 and 2007 went to the wealthiest 1 percent of society and that income for the top 1 percent grew 10 times faster than that of the bottom 90 percent. Piketty and Saez found that the top 1 percent of earners got a higher share of income in 2007 than at any time since 1928.

The latest figures come amid constant calls by the White House and Congress to cut social programs in order to balance the budget. The federal government, we are told, has been bankrupted by the "profligacy" of social programs and the proportion of social resources allocated to the general population.

But the latest figures show that the opposite is true. It is the rich who have bankrupted the state, with the full assistance of the two big-business parties.

12

Current High Tax Rates for the Wealthy Have Created Class Divisions

Brian T. Carter

Brian T. Carter is a writer for American Thinker.

Around the world and even among the American poor, Scrooge McDuck—a Disney character—provides a portrait of a stereotypical rich person. The prevailing thought is that because Scrooge McDuck does not really need his money, there seems to be no reason why he should not give it away. In fact, many poor become angry when the wealthy refuse to give them money. Likewise, many Americans believe that taxing the wealthy will solve every economic problem. Unfortunately, the view that rich Americans should be taxed at a higher rate has created class divisions.

On a sidewalk in Monterrey, Mexico—a rich (by Mexican standards) industrial city in the northern state of Nuevo Leon—a kid, reasonably well-dressed with clean clothes and flip-flops, approaches an American and asks, "Por favor, usted me da dinero para la escuela?" (Will you please give me money for school?)

In southern Mexico, a 6-year-old—without any clothes—approaches an American, "Usted puede darme dinero para comer?" (Can you give me money to eat?)

In the Kabul [Afghanistan] Green Zone, a clean-cut boy in a new school uniform—dark blue slacks with a light blue polo shirt—catches up to some Americans walking between bases. With some shock, one American realizes this is the same boy who, just yesterday, was caked in dirt and wearing tattered clothes while begging for a dollar.

In Manila [Philippines], kids offer to serve as guides, sell flowers, flag down a taxi for pesos, or just beg. Their poverty runs the gamut from well-dressed, well fed, and clean; to fed and relatively clean-cut kids wearing torn hand-me downs in the squatter areas; to filthy, near feral looking pre-teens without any clothes whatsoever.

One consistency is their view of foreigners—Americans, Europeans, Japanese, and Koreans—as wealthy beyond imagination. Foreigners are so wealthy, many are offended—or even angry—if the foreigners fail to leave a trail of money.

Why do these children feel foreigners owe them money?

Scrooge McDuck.

The Legacy of Scrooge McDuck

Scrooge McDuck is wealthy. Thanks to Disney's distribution, Donald's rich uncle is known the world over. Everybody knows about McDuck's multi-story vault with a diving board, and how he literally "dives in," swimming through his fortune of gold bars, silver coins, and hundred dollar bills.

> The challenge is the McDuck view of wealth is not restricted to poor kids in the third world.

The money is just sitting there. Never mind Scrooge McDuck earned the money; he isn't using it, so McDuck doesn't need it. In fact, McDuck would still be rich if he gave over half of it away to those who really need it—like kids in Mexico, the Philippines, and Afghanistan. Obviously, the rich foreigners, like McDuck, are selfish jerks for not sharing their "luck."

Reasonable adults can forgive the naiveté of poorly educated kids who don't understand finance. Educated people know [Microsoft's] Bill Gates, [filmmaker] Steven Spielberg, [investor] Warren Buffett, [investor] George Soros, and [business magnate] Mike Bloomberg don't go swimming through their wealth in a high-rise vault like McDuck. Their money is invested; their wealth is primarily on paper. If the celebrity super-rich ever tried to liquidate their assets, much of the value would evaporate before they could click "sell." Even selling a small percentage of their holdings could cause key stocks to collapse, impact the wider market, and result in real—not paper—layoffs.

The challenge is the McDuck view of wealth is not restricted to poor kids in the third world. Aggressive panhandlers in San Francisco have been demonstrating an entitlement mentality for decades. These beggars target anybody who looks like they have a steady job, regardless of whether they are independently wealthy or working poor. The aggressive begging is a soft terrorism—"give me money and I won't act crazy threatening you"—justified by the beggar's belief they are owed something by anybody with a job. After all, in the mind of the beggar, the only difference between themselves, the working stiff, and the rich kid sporting a silver spoon is "luck."

Resenting the Rich

Far worse, the "rich are McDuck" worldview infected middle class America. A systems engineer earning $100,000/year near Dallas remarked in late November 2008, ". . .it's time the rich start paying their fair share; poor people need help." For this Dallas engineer, anyone making over $250,000 a year is Scrooge McDuck, swimming through a fortune of hoarded loot. The fact productive Americans transferred over $15 trillion in wealth to the poor since 1964 is irrelevant. He is totally ignorant of real poverty where kids lack basic clothing and can't bathe. The "poor" of Dallas—like most American poor—have cars, cable TV, computers, smart phones, and are, more likely than not, overweight.

This engineer doesn't see himself as wealthy. He doesn't realize, an office manager making only $50,000 a year sees the engineer as McDuck. In turn, a person living in public housing likely sees anybody above their station as Scrooge McDuck, sitting on more money than they know what to do with, selfish to the core, winners in life's lottery.

The McDuck view of wealth is static and only sees money as physical. These poorly educated people don't understand money stuffed in a mattress loses value through inflation. They don't understand invested money increases in value, grows jobs, and creates more opportunity for everybody.

For people who believe wealth and opportunity are simply the results of a birth lottery, what is the incentive to work harder? They are zombies, feasting off the productive. For the zombies, people who earn more are not paying their fair share. In the McDuck worldview, to advance, others must be pulled down. This mindset explains why "taxing the rich" is a nonnegotiable demand of their leaders, even when history shows increasing tax rates lowers tax revenue, while lowering tax rates historically increases tax revenue.

As [conservative commentator] Mark Levin says, they are drones.

Preventing Class Divisions

Listen to Ronald Reagan's 1981 inaugural address where he explains the injustice of the tax system, "Those who do work are denied a fair return for their labor by a tax system which penalizes successful achievement and keeps us from maintaining full productivity." Reagan understood how wealth was created. Instead of dividing citizens along class lines, stoking anger and fomenting envy with talk of "fair shares," Reagan—

throughout the speech—appealed to all Americans with a vision of increasing prosperity shared by all.

In his farewell address, George Washington spoke at length about the importance of uniting America. Washington also counseled Americans "it is essential that public opinion should be enlightened," and the "general diffusion of knowledge" is "an object of primary importance" because of public opinion's influence on government. When the citizenry learns all they know about finance from Disney cartoons, the Republic is threatened.

Breaking up the class divisions requires debunking the McDuck mythology and educating Americans about wealth, wealth creation, and how wealth creates jobs. Like Reagan, any future leader who hopes to reunite the country, must offer a vision of shared prosperity, instead of shared misery and revenge.

13

You Can't Tax the Rich

Thomas Sowell

Thomas Sowell is a senior fellow at the Hoover Institution.

In an earlier era, the federal government raised taxes so high, the rich simply moved their money into safe havens where it could not be taxed. Unfortunately, many politicians in our current era seem determined to repeat history. The downside of these policies is that they hurt the American economy and promote class warfare. If the tax rate rises, the rich will simply seek out tax havens as they have in the past.

Ninety years ago—in 1921—federal income-tax policies reached an absurdity that many people today seem to want to repeat. Those who believe in high taxes on "the rich" got their way. The tax rate on people in the top income bracket was 73 percent in 1921. On the other hand, the rich also got their way: They didn't actually pay those taxes.

The number of people with taxable incomes of $300,000 a year or more—equivalent to far more than $1 million in today's money—declined from over 1,000 people in 1916 to fewer than 300 in 1921. Were the rich all going broke?

It might look that way. More than four-fifths of the total taxable income earned by people making $300,000 a year and up vanished into thin air. So did the tax revenues that the government hoped to collect with high tax rates on the top incomes.

What happened was no mystery to Secretary of the Treasury Andrew Mellon. He pointed out that vast amounts of money that might have been invested in the economy were instead being invested in tax-exempt securities, such as municipal bonds.

Secretary Mellon estimated that the amount of money invested in tax-exempt securities had nearly tripled in a decade. The amount of this money that the tax collector couldn't touch was larger than the federal government's annual budget and nearly half as large as the national debt. Big bucks went into hiding.

Mellon highlighted the absurdity of this situation: "It is incredible that a system of taxation which permits a man with an income of $1,000,000 a year to pay not one cent to the support of his Government should remain unaltered."

If anything, "the rich" have far more options for putting their money beyond the reach of the tax collectors today than they had back in 1921.

One of Mellon's first acts as secretary was to ask Congress to end tax exemptions for municipal bonds and other securities. But Congress was not about to set off a political firestorm by doing that.

Mellon's Plan B was to cut the top income-tax rate, in order to lure money out of tax-exempt securities and back into the economy, where increased economic activity would generate more tax revenue for the government. Congress also resisted this, using arguments that are virtually unchanged to this day—that these would just be "tax cuts for the rich."

Repeating History

What makes all this history so relevant today is that the same economic assumptions and political arguments that produced the absurdities of 1921 are still going strong in 2011.

If anything, "the rich" have far more options for putting their money beyond the reach of the tax collectors today than they had back in 1921. In addition to being able to put their money into tax-exempt securities, the rich today can easily send millions—or billions—of dollars to foreign countries, with the ease of electronic transfers in a globalized economy.

Class-warfare politics pays off in votes for politicians who can depict their opponents as defenders of the rich and themselves as champions of the working people.

In other words, the genuinely rich are likely to be the least harmed by high tax rates in the top brackets. People who are looking for jobs are likely to be the most harmed, because they cannot equally easily transfer themselves overseas to take the jobs that are being created there by American investments that are fleeing high tax rates at home.

Small businesses—hardware stores, gas stations, restaurants—are likewise unable to transfer themselves overseas. So they are far more likely to be unable to escape the higher tax rates that are supposedly being imposed on "millionaires and billionaires," as President Obama calls them. Moreover, small businesses are what create most of the new jobs.

Class Warfare

Why then are so many politicians, journalists, and others so gung-ho to raise tax rates on the rich?

Aside from sheer ignorance of history and economics, class-warfare politics pays off in votes for politicians who can depict their opponents as defenders of the rich and themselves as champions of the working people. It is a great political game that has paid off repeatedly in local, state, and federal elections.

As for the 1920s, Mellon eventually got his way, getting Congress to bring the top income-tax rate down from 73 percent to 24 percent. Vast sums of money that had seemingly vanished into thin air suddenly reappeared in the economy, creating far more jobs and far more tax revenue for the government.

Sometimes sanity prevails. But not always.

Organizations to Contact

The editors have compiled the following list of organizations concerned with the issues debated in this book. The descriptions are derived from materials provided by the organizations. All have publications or information available for interested readers. The list was compiled on the date of publication of the present volume; the information provided here may change. Be aware that many organizations take several weeks or longer to respond to inquiries, so allow as much time as possible.

American Enterprise Institute (AEI)
1150 Seventeenth St. NW, Washington, DC 20036
(202) 862-5800 • fax: (202) 862-7177
website: www.aei.org

The American Enterprise Institute (AEI) is a conservative think tank, founded in 1943 to defend the principles and improve the institutions of American freedom and democratic capitalism. AEI promotes limited government, private enterprise, individual liberty and responsibility, vigilant and effective defense and foreign policies, political accountability, and open debate. Economic policy is one of AEI's research areas and its website is a source of many books and publications relating to the US economy. Recent articles include, for example, "Recession Blues" and "What Is Fiscally—and Politically—Sustainable?"

Brookings Institution
1775 Massachusetts Ave. NW, Washington, DC 20036
(202) 797-6000
website: www.brookings.edu

The Brookings Institution is a nonprofit public policy organization whose mission is to conduct high-quality, independent research and provide innovative, practical recommendations that advance three broad goals: (1) strengthening American democracy; (2) fostering the economic and social welfare, security, and opportunity of all Americans; and (3) securing a more open, safe, prosperous, and cooperative international system. The group's website contains a section on the economy, where numerous publications on the current recession can be found. Two recent examples include "The US Financial and Economic Crisis: Where Does It Stand and Where Do We Go from Here?" and "Financial Globalization and Economic Policies."

Cato Institute

1000 Massachusetts Ave. NW, Washington, DC   20001-5403
(202) 842-0200 • fax: (202) 842-3490
website: www.cato.org

The Cato Institute is a nonprofit public policy research foundation known for its libertarian viewpoints. The foundation's mission is to increase the understanding of public policies based on the principles of limited government, free markets, individual liberty, and peace. The group's website provides an extensive list of publications dealing with various public policy issues, including economic matters. Cato also publishes papers in the *Cato Journal* three times per year, the quarterly magazine *Regulation*, and a bimonthly newsletter, *Cato Policy Report*. Recent publications include "The Limits of Monetary Policy" and "Monetary Policy and Financial Regulation."

Citizens for Tax Justice (CTJ)

1616 P St. NW, Suite 200, Washington, DC   20036
(202) 299-1066 • fax: (202) 299-1065
website: www.ctj.org

Citizens for Tax Justice (CTJ) is a research and advocacy organization that seeks to give all citizens a voice in the debates about tax policy. It promotes tax policy that is fair for low- and middle-income Americans, that requires wealthy Americans to pay their fair share, that closes corporate loopholes, that funds important government services, that reduces the federal debt, and that minimizes the distortion of economic markets. CTJ's publications include *Tax Justice Digest* and policy statements such as *A Progressive Solution to the AMT Problem*.

Economic Policy Institute (EPI)

1333 H St. NW, Suite 300, East Tower
Washington, DC 20005-4707
(202) 775-8810 • fax: (202) 775-0819
e-mail: researchdept@epi.org
website: www.epi.org

The Economic Policy Institute (EPI) is a nonprofit Washington, DC, think tank created in 1986 to broaden the discussion about economic policy to include the interests of low- and middle-income workers. The group conducts research on the status of American workers and publishes a report called "State of Working America" every two years. The EPI website provides a list of publications, many of which concern US economic matters. Examples of publications include "Worst Downturn Since the Great Depression" and "Too Big to Fail . . . and Getting Bigger."

The Federal Reserve System

20th St. and Constitution Ave. NW, Washington, DC 20551
website: www.federalreserve.gov

The Federal Reserve System was created by Congress in 1913 to be the nation's central bank. It is made up of a seven-member Board of Governors, a twelve-member Federal Open Market Committee, twelve regional member banks located throughout the United States, and staff economists. The Federal Reserve's function is to control inflation without triggering a recession. In addition, the Federal Reserve supervises the nation's banking system to protect consumers; maintains the stability of the financial markets to prevent potential crises; and acts as the Central Bank for other banks, the US Government, and foreign banks. The Federal Reserve's website is a source of economic research and data and consumer financial information.

The Heritage Foundation

214 Massachusetts Ave. NE, Washington, DC   20002-4999
(202) 546-4400 • fax: (202) 546-8328
website: www.heritage.org

The Heritage Foundation is a conservative public policy research institute founded in 1973 whose mission is to formulate and promote conservative public policies based on the principles of free enterprise, limited government, individual freedom, traditional American values, and a strong national defense. The economy is one of the institute's primary concerns and its website is a source of economic publications such as "Republicans' Financial Regulatory Reform Plan a Good Start" and "Government Intervention: A Threat to Economic Recovery."

National Bureau of Economic Research (NBER)

1050 Massachusetts Ave., Cambridge, MA   02138-5398
(617) 868-3900 • fax: (617) 868-2742
website: www.nber.org

Founded in 1920, the National Bureau of Economic Research (NBER) is a private, nonprofit, nonpartisan research organization that undertakes unbiased economic research among public policy makers, business professionals, and the academic community. A search of the NBER website produces numerous working papers and other information on various economic issues, including the 2009 recession. Examples of recent publications include "The Credit Rating Crisis" and "Inflation and the Stock Market: Understanding the 'Fed Model.'"

The Tax Foundation

529 14th St. NW, Suite 420, Washington, DC   20045-1000
(202) 464-6200 • fax: (202) 464-6201
e-mail: tf@taxfoundation.org
website: www.taxfoundation.org

The Tax Foundation is a nonpartisan tax research organization that educates taxpayers about tax policy and the current tax burden. It promotes a tax policy that is simple, transparent, stable, neutral, and that promotes growth. The Foundation publishes *Fiscal Facts*, the *Tax Watch* and *Tax Features* newsletters, books such as *A Taxpayer's Guide to Federal Spending*, and many other publications.

US Department of the Treasury
1500 Pennsylvania Ave. NW, Washington, DC   20220
(202) 622-2000 • fax: (202) 622-6415
website: www.ustreas.gov

The US Department of the Treasury is the executive agency responsible for promoting economic prosperity and ensuring the financial security of the United States. The entity is responsible for a wide range of activities, such as advising the president on economic and financial issues, encouraging sustainable economic growth, and fostering improved governance in financial institutions. The Treasury Department's website is a source of news and other information about the US economy, including various government initiatives, such as the Emergency Economic Stabilization Act—Troubled Asset Relief Program (TARP) and other actions being taken to combat economic recession in the United States.

Bibliography

Books

Daron Acemoglu and James Robinson — *Why Nations Fail: The Origins of Power, Prosperity, and Poverty.* New York: Crown Business, 2012.

Bruce Bartlett — *The Benefit and the Burden: Tax Reform—Why We Need It and What It Will Take.* New York: Simon and Schuster, 2012.

Leonard E. Burman and Joel Slemrod — *Taxes in America: What Everyone Needs to Know.* New York: Oxford University, 2012.

Nicholas Eberstadt — *A Nation of Takers: America's Entitlement Epidemic.* West Conshohocken, PA: Templeton, 2012.

Al Gore — *The Future: Six Drivers of Global Change.* New York: Random House, 2013.

Ken Hoagland — *The Fair Tax Solution: Financial Justice for All Americans.* New York: Sentinel, 2010.

Stephen Moore — *Who's the Fairest of Them All? The Truth About Opportunity, Taxes, and Wealth in America.* Jackson, TN: Encounter, 2012.

Nouriel Roubini — *Crisis Economics.* New York: Allen Lane, 2010.

Peter D. Schiff   *The Real Crash: America's Coming Bankruptcy—How to Save Yourself and Your Country*. New York: St. Martin's, 2012.

Tavis Smiley and Cornel West   *The Rich and the Rest of Us: A Poverty Manifesto*. Carlsbad, CA: Smiley Books, 2012.

Thomas Sowell   *Trickle Down Theory and Tax Cuts for the Rich*. Chicago: Hoover Institution, 2012.

Charles J. Sykes   *A Nation of Moochers: America's Addiction to Getting Something for Nothing*. New York: St. Martin's, 2012.

Peter J. Tanous and Jeff Cox   *Debt, Deficits, and the Demise of the American Economy*. Hoboken, NJ: Wiley, 2011.

Joseph J. Thorndike   *Their Fair Share: Taxing the Rich in the Age of FDR*. Washington, DC: Urban Institute, 2013.

Daniel Wessel   *Red Ink: Inside High-Stakes Politics of the Federal Budget*. New York: Crown, 2012.

Periodicals and Internet Sources

Huzaima Bukhari and Ikramul Haq   "Tax Amnesty for Whom?" *Business Recorder*, January 11, 2013.

Business Recorder   "Amnesty Schemes Not for 'Super Rich,'" December 29, 2012.

Economist	"Waiting for the Chop," March 2, 2013.
Brian Farmer	"Is Soaking the Rich the Right Answer?" *New American*, March 4, 2013.
Financial Express	"Mr. Rich, Please Do Not Die," February 15, 2013.
Financial Express	"Rich Don't Get Richer, No One Gets Poorer," March 1, 2013.
Financial Express	"To Prosperity or Perdition?" February 28, 2013.
Kevin A. Hassett	"The Progressive U.S. Tax Code," *National Review*, January 28, 2013.
Billy House	"Middle Ground on Tax Hike on the Rich Sought," *National Journal*, December 7, 2012.
Denis Kleinfeld	"Tax the Rich Foundations, Not the 'Rich,'" *Newsmax*, December 17, 2012. www.newsmax.com.
Maclean's	"Closing Ranks," February 11, 2013.
Robert Reich and John Lott	"Should the Rich Pay Higher Taxes?" *New York Times Upfront*, February 18, 2013.
Matthew Rothschild	"Obama, the Hang-Glider," *Progressive*, February 2013.

Veronique de Rugy	"Soaking the Rich: Sorry, Warren Buffett, but Extracting Cash from the Wealthy Won't Solve Our Problems," *Reason*, March 2013.
Gil Weinreich	"Kill Your 401(k), Conservative Author Says," *Advisor One*, March 14, 2013.
Gil Weinreich	"Tax-Weary U.S. Millionaires Embrace Cayman Islands, Hong Kong for Relief," *Advisor One*, March 13, 2013.
Gil Weinreich	"What Do We Do as the Rich Get Richer," *Advisor One*, February 15, 2013.
Armstrong Williams	"A Wealthy Tax Would Hurt the Economy," *Newsmax*, December 31, 2012. www.newsmax.com.
Graeme Wood	"Who Are the Millionaires? Little Unites Them Other than That They Are Tax Targets," *National Review*, December 31, 2012.
Amy Woods	"Issa: America at Risk of Losing Economic Power," *Newsmax*, December 30, 2012. www.newsmax.com.

Index